The Art of the Hustle

Lessons in Becoming a Man

Jo Evans Lynn

&

Council of Elders

This1Matters Foundation, Greensboro, NC, 27406

Second Edition Published by:

This1Matters Foundation, Greensboro, NC, 27406

ISBN: 978-1-7369837-4-4

Council of Elders

Elder Thomas Alan Bell

Elder Ezekiel Ben-Israel

Elder Timothy E. "Gene" Blackmon

Elder Larry C. Burnett

Elder McArthur Davis

Elder Milton "Choo Choo" Grady

Elder Arthur Johnson, Jr.

Lt. Col./Retired Clifton Girard Johnson

Rev. Alphonso McGlen

Elder Ralph D. Mitchell

Elder David "Bunny" Moore

Elder Robert "Bob" Purvis

Elder James Aquilla Smith

Elder Henry "Hank" Wall

Elder John E. Wynn

Dedication

This book is dedicated to our grandfathers, our fathers, our uncles, our coaches, and the other men in our lives who fathered us and mentored us from boyhood to manhood.

Acknowledgements

We would like to acknowledge our mothers, our grandmothers, our wives, and the mothers of our children who have helped make our houses homes and our children well nurtured and self-actualizing adults.

The Council of Elders would like to thank Larry D. Donnell the owner of Africa & More at 1004 West Gate City Boulevard, Greensboro for so graciously providing the authentic African attire and canes for the Elder's portraits and cover picture.

We also thank Mr. Fuse Green for so generously using his outstanding talent as a graphic artist to design our logo.

Preface

The term "hustle" has changed in meaning through the years. Back in the day when fathering a child was a commitment to taking an active role in rearing the child, "hustling" meant doing what it took to provide for one's family. Although the hustle entailed hard work and often manual labor, it included so much more.

Hustling also meant doing what it took to stay alive and with one's family. In the South, this also meant, for Black boys and men, mastering certain mannerisms and behaviors. It was the unspoken duty of the men in the community to teach their sons, nephews, and fatherless neighbors the "art of the hustle."

The men whose stories are included here had fathers, grandfathers, uncles, teachers, coaches, and church members who made sure they knew what they needed to know. Most of them have raised sons of their own and mentored young men in their neighborhoods, schools, communities, and churches.

The purpose of this book is to ensure that present and future generations of African American males have the skills and tools they need to survive and develop into nurturing fathers and self-actualizing citizens.

Table of Contents

The Hustling Begins at an Early Age

The Spirit of a Mentor

Elder "Bunny" David Moore

I went to work with my father at the age of twelve. My mother wasn't in favor of it. She loved to "baby up" her children, but my father wasn't having it.

My father and his brother had learned to do gardening work from their father when they were around that age. Both of his parents understood what hard work was all about. His mother was a beautician, but she gave that up to open her own store in

Lincoln Grove. The first floor of the building was a grocery store, and she rented out rooms on the second floor. In other words, everyone in the family worked.

My father told my mother, "A man needs to know how to work. He needs to know how to provide for his family." My father was a quiet man. He didn't say much, but when he spoke his word was law in our house.

So, I went to work with him. It wasn't easy work like people sometimes give kids- like picking up sticks doing more playing than working. When I started, it was just my father and me. I cut the grass, and my father did all of the digging, planting, edging the lawns, and trimming rose bushes. When we were working, he was as hard as, maybe harder, on me than he would have been on other workers. No one-half stepped on the job. Anyone who worked for my father did the job right. By the early 2000s, five generations of my family had been employed as gardeners in the Greensboro area. I guess that's why even years later, being able to tell a probable employer that you learned gardening or landscaping from my father was the surest way to get the job.

My father was the best gardener and landscaper in Greensboro, North Carolina. I'm not just saying that. He won all kinds of awards and his gardens, especially his roses, were featured in the newspaper and even in a big-time magazine. All the rich White folks in those mansions out in Irving Park wanted him to work for them. He took great pride in his work.

Often, after another article came out about his beautiful roses, people would offer him as much as $500.00 a week to come and work for them, but he was loyal to his longtime customers. He could afford to be selective with his clients. I remember an important lesson that I learned about how he selected and kept his clients.

****

One time, shortly after I started working with my father, we were working in this rich lady's garden. She brought some members of her garden club out to see the garden. She pointed my Dad out sayings, "David is the best yard boy in Greensboro."

First, I thought that maybe she had mistaken me for my Dad, but then I realized that she couldn't see me because I was behind a fountain. It made me mad her calling my Dad a "Yard Boy." I was the only "boy" out there, and I didn't much care for that term for myself because I was already doing a man's work.

Dad didn't say anything. He just kept digging around some plants. I wanted him to say something. I wanted him to bless her out and walk off the job.

He just nodded his head when one of the women that were with her complimented his roses.

The next week, when it was the day to go to that lady's garden, I expected my Dad to drive right on by.

He didn't.

He went in and worked just like he always did. When he noticed that I was acting kind of slack-half cutting the grass- he said, "Don't make me take a switch to you boy. Do like I taught you to do."

When it was time for me to go up to the house and collect the check, Dad said, "I'll go."

I watched expecting him to tell the lady that we wouldn't be back. When she tried to give him a check, he looked at it, shook his head, and handed it back to her. I couldn't hear what he said, but the lady fussed a while, but then went back into the house and came out with another check. Dad looked at it, nodded, turned around and walked back to the truck.

He didn't say a word. He just handed me the check. My eyes about popped out of my head. The check was for two times as much as he usually charged and instead of being made out to David Moore it was made out to Mr. David Moore. It made sense. A yard "boy" cost that lady twice as much as a gardener, and there was no mistaking Mr. David Moore for a "boy."

The lesson that I learned was that when you're really good at what you do, you can demand respect.

That was just one of the lessons that I learned from my father about being a provider and hustling to take care of the family. My father, like most of the men of his generation, had more than one job. Most of the men had big families, and wages were low. My family was kind of small with only seven kids. On the weekends, my father usually worked as a bartender at parties. He was in almost as much demand as a bartender as he was a gardener. I remember one time someone paid him extra plus his fare to go to Charleston, South Carolina to tend the bar at a man's daughter's wedding reception.

With Dad working all the time, that left most of the nurturing of us children to my mother. I knew that my father loved me, but it wasn't his way to say, "I love you son." He didn't even smile and compliment me when I had done a good job. He'd just look over the job, nod his head, and tell me what to do next. Something was missing, but I didn't know what it was until later in life when I listened to other men talk about their relationships with their fathers.

My mother was the nurturer. She loved her children, and she loved to take care of everyone. I guess that is why the ingrained desire to help others began with me before I was born. I come from a family of caring people. It, caring about people and wanting to make a difference, began with my mother telling me about how my grandmother and grandfather took care of the people in the community. Granddaddy was a preacher. Back then, the preacher was often the best-educated person in the community. He served in many roles from counselor to comforter. Grand-daddy and grandma would also put together baskets and take them to the sick and elderly and my mother, who was a young girl at the time, would go with them.

I began working on my theory about helping people when I was young. I believed and still believe to this day, that the more people I know; the more people I can help. They call it networking now. Back in the day, I just called it being a friend to everyone I met.

With me, the spirit of giving back developed with being in the Sunshine Band in the church. My mother was over the Sunshine Band, and all the children of the church had to be in it. As one of the oldest boys in my community, that naturally made me the leader of most any group that I was in. I was pretty good at basketball too- I could jump and guard the tallest player on the other team. So, I was usually the captain on the team. I guess I've been a leader all my life. That role along with my desire to help others set me on the road to mentoring.

Whenever a group of men gets together, especially men who have sons, they talk about how they raised their sons. They would say, "I did this"… or "My father told me that"… All of us learned so much from each other. The one thing I regret most in life is that by the time I started working with other men to mentor boys, my son was ready grown.

For me, mentoring started with a small group of men who wanted to "save" the boys in our community. We knew that the 1980s and the arrival of the drug epidemic had done a number on communities like the ones that we had grown up in. The nurturing "villages" of our childhoods no longer existed for many children. Several of the men in the group had young sons of their own. We learned from each other. Some of us had had fathers in the home, and some hadn't. Even those, like me, who had fathers in the home were fathered differently than they wanted their sons raised.

We had learned our fathers' concept of what a "real" man was supposed to do and how a real man was supposed to act. A real man didn't cry. A real man didn't show his emotions. We wanted to leave that part of the real man concept behind, but to keep the basics of working, being a provider and such. We wanted to teach the boys that emotional closeness was part of being a real man. Most of us couldn't remember ever hearing our father say, "I love you." And no one could remember getting a hug- just because.

We wanted the boys that we mentored to understand that fathers and other male role models could be strong, supportive, and emotionally connected. Hank Wall and I started working with kids at Hayes-Taylor YMCA. We called it the Y's Men. Later, around 1993, we got with some other guys who wanted to make a difference in the community-Sam Rhodes and Reggie Gaines, who both worked at Hayes Taylor YMCA. Hank came up with the name Brothers Organized to Save Others (BOTSO). Bob McAdoo, who was playing with the Los Angeles Lakers at the time, was an honorary member of BOTSO. We started at three elementary schools -Washington Street School, and Hampton Elementary School in Greensboro, North Carolina and Fairview Elementary School in High Point, North Carolina.

I was the first president or leader of the group. Sam and I were in charge of putting the programs and activities together. We didn't have much money so we had what we called a PATH Fund. We'd *pass around the hat* and collect money any place folks gathered. Since people knew what we were trying to do, the hat always came back with plenty of money. We also had what we called our OOOOP fund (Out of our own pockets) to help finance our activities.

BOTSO added several new mentors like John Wynn, Curtis Douglas, Milton Grady, and Patrick Faulkner and evolved into MenTors in 2005. Our theme was: Faith, Family, Education, and Community. Our mission was to be men mentoring young men. By 2015, we were mostly grandfathers with different roles in our families and communities-we were elders. However, our roles as mentors never changed. As the Council of Elders, we expanded our mentoring to include more of the school's that serve as feeder schools to James B. Dudley High School- one of the last historically Black high schools left in North Carolina.

Sometimes we tutored, but most of the time we just talked with the kids. For example, if a teacher had a student standing out in the hall for punishment, we would ask if it was all right for one of us to talk to the child. Most of the time it was a matter of listening more than talking. It's surprising how many children just want someone, an adult, to talk to them like they are somebody. Usually, after a little time the child would return to the classroom and be just fine.

All of my years mentoring have been rewarding, but the years with BOTSO were especially rewarding- I guess because we were pioneers in mentoring African American males. We started out with five major projects: The Aggie Eagle Classic, University Day at North Carolina A&T State University, A Sleepover at the beginning of the school year, A Special Trip to give the young men an opportunity to do something they had never done like White Water Rafting, Skiing, or visiting Washington D.C., and another Sleepover at the end of the school year.

We also were the first to start Midnight Basketball in Greensboro. BOSTO was also one of the first groups in Greensboro to get involved in the Million Man Movement and we participated in the March on Washington D.C. We were one of twenty-two busloads of men from the Greensboro area that participated in the march.

We received many awards from state and local governments, but to me, the greatest reward is having some of the 3,000-4,000 young men that I mentored over the last thirty years come back and say, "You made a difference in my life. I don't know where I would have been today if you had not been there for me."

Logo design by Fuse Green

A Brief History of the Council of Elders

The Council of Elders evolved over a period of more than twenty years from the four founding members of Brothers Organized to Save Others (BOTSO): David "Bunny" Moore, Henry "Hank" Wall, Sam Rhodes, and Reggie Gaines and first additions John Wynn, Curtis Douglas, Patrick Faulkner, and Milton Grady. In 2005, the group incorporated and became MenTors, Inc., and in 2015 the group made its final metamorphosis to the Council of Elders. Throughout the years, the mission has remained the same: We are men mentoring young men from boyhood to manhood. We want them to become men of character that are skilled, well-educated providers emotionally connected to their families, to their community, and to their culture.

We want our young men to understand the true nature of fatherhood-that a good father corrects, comforts, instructs, and provides for the needs of his children and that a great father teaches his children about their heavenly Father. Our goal is to help build strong families and communities led by Black men who are informed and empowered to be able and willing to mentor future generations.

The Village

Lessons in Community

Elder Henry "Hank" Wall

I can remember Friday evenings during the fall as a young boy in High Point, North Carolina living on Hay Street.

My Dad, Ray Armstrong, Floyd Kirby, my uncles, and The Clinton Boys, they would go hunting. At about 5:00 o'clock on Friday, they'd have about five cars lined up.

You'd see these men coming out of the houses with hunting bags on their shoulders. They had ammo in the hunting bags, and they would have shotguns. They'd be heading to what they called "down home" to Wadesboro to get the meat for the week. They were going hunting.

Either that night or mostly the next night, Saturday night, they would come back. My dad usually would have four or five rabbits and some squirrels. We'd spend the evening skinning and cleaning rabbits and squirrels. We didn't have a television.

If someone had gotten more than they needed, they'd share with the others. We would take care of each other. My family didn't need much because it was just me, my dad, and my mom. I was the only child at home. I had two sisters, but they were older and were grown and gone.

The man I call my father, Mr. Jacob Wall, was actually my uncle. He was born in Anson County North Carolina one of 14 children. His father was a sharecropper. When I was three months old, he and his wife Odessa took me in and raised me as though I was their natural born son. You see, my Aunt Odessa's sister Mary (my natural mother) gave birth to me when she was 15 years old. I've been told that my biological father, Jesse James, a “pool hustler/plasterer, ran down from the pool room on Washington Street in High Point to see me when I was born. I was delivered in my grandmother’s house by Ms. Carter the local mid-wife.

I was named Henry Adams Bennett. I did not see my biological father again until I was nine years old. He didn’t turn up after that until my senior class took a field trip to Washington D.C. where he lived. I later found out that he was pretty famous in D.C. for being one of the best plasterers in the city. He worked on many of the historical sites in the D.C. and Virginia areas.

I thought of Jacob Wall as my “real” dad. He worked two jobs most of his life. He worked at Melrose Hosiery Mill and did lawns on the weekend in the rich white section of High Point called Emerywood. Sometimes, when I was about ten years old, I would help him with the lawn work. That didn’t last long because I was slowing him down. So, he just left me at home and got someone older if he needed help. Since he had grown up on a farm, he knew all about soil and could make anything grow.

My other "real" Dad was my stepfather Postell Adams. He already had four boys when he married my mother, Mary. They had 11 children together. He was a good, hard working man and always treated me as though I was one of his own children. I think I ate at his house almost as often as I ate at my own home. He took an interest in me and often came to see me play basketball at William Penn High School. That's just how it was back then; every child was a welcome addition to the family no matter the circumstances of their birth.

Another special thing about growing up in the "village" was the way we did church. I could walk to my church from my house. It was only about two blocks away. It was called Olga Avenue Church of Christ. In fact, from the time I was five to about nine years old my church held services at my grandma's house. About that time, they got up enough money to buy a parcel of land to build a church. One of the men in the neighborhood was a brick mason- he supervised the construction, but it was the men in the church who did most of the actual building. I can remember, as a small boy, handing the men bricks and rolling the wheelbarrow with the sand. It wasn't just the contractor and his crew who did the work. All the men in the church helped supply the manpower inside and out- carpentry work, painting, and such.

I remember being excited about the church being out of my grandma's house and about the fact that we had a real church building. Though I was only nine years old, I saw the people working together to get something done.

When the church was completed, we went to revivals all over the state- Winston Salem, Rock Hill, Statesville, Salisbury, Concord, Kannapolis, and Greensboro. All the black churches, during that time, supported each other during the summertime. It was what they called the Revival Season. Once we had a church building, we could be part of that circuit. For example, if we were going to Rock Hill, the men would line up about five or six cars, and everyone would pile in wherever they had room. A church family was just that way.

You heard me say that I was the only child at home, but I grew up as part of two families. In my house, I was raised as an only child, but we all went together to one church. When the cars lined up to go somewhere, it didn't matter which car you got in. In a church family, usually, a lot of the members were "blood" relatives. We would go everywhere five or six cars "deep." That's how I learned to drive. I learned early not to allow anyone to cut in. There weren't any superhighways-just two lanes, but nobody was ever allowed to cut in on any of the cars. All of these things transferred to me and out of all my brothers, five of them, ended up being truck drivers. All of them drove eighteen wheelers- I didn't want any part of that, but I could have. That was part of the village- having the skills to choose.

Also, we lived in the same neighborhood with all the people who had important roles in the community. We lived in an apartment. We lived right next door to the medicine woman. Her name was Mama Annie. She was probably in her sixties when I was around nine years old. Anytime anyone got sick in the neighborhood, they'd call on Mama Annie, and she'd tell them what to do to get rid of the sickness or fever or whatever.

So, I was fortunate enough to live right next door to her. Anytime I got sick she would take care of me. Sometimes she would send me and my best friend, Shelton, to go out into the woods to get herbs that she would describe to us. I can remember Catnip to this day. Things like that we liked to chew on. So, I was gathering herbs at a young age. Any time of the day or night Mama Annie was there to help people.

The children belonged to every adult in the neighborhood. I remember one time a friend and I got in trouble. You didn't see hardly any white people in the neighborhood. Only two white people came into the neighborhood- one was the insurance man, and the other one was the Raleigh Man- he had the liniment, and flavorings for cooking.

One day, my partner and I decided that we would "rock" the Raleigh Man. So, we threw rocks at him and chased him to his car. We rocked his car and messed around and broke one of his windows. Naturally, we didn't do it in front of our own house, but one of the neighbor ladies saw us, and she called us into her house and whipped us. Then the phone call beat us home, and our parents whipped us. That's the way the village operated.

A lot of what went on in the neighborhood, we didn't find out about until later in life. The street where I lived, Hay Street, ran north and south and Hoover Street ran east and west. I didn't find out until I was a grown man that Hoover Street's nickname was Bomber Row because it had so many liquor houses up and down the street.

At the time of my youth, the ambulance was the hearse from the Black funeral home. They'd come and pick up the wounded. The same vehicle that took the dead people away took the hurt people to the hospital that got messed up on the weekend. My friends and I would just hang out, especially in the summertime, and follow the ambulance to see what was going on in the neighborhood.

Just because there was drinking and a little bit of action on the weekend didn't make it a bad place to live. I had my third, fourth, and fifth-grade teachers living on the same street. The principal of William Penn High School lived on the next street right behind me. There was the whole village right there living in one place.

So, you had the factory workers, teachers, principals, and liquor houses all in one place. I guess by today's standards we were all some degree of poor. Although teachers, ministers, and business owners lived alongside us, they were not that much wealthier than the rest of us. In most cases, the degree of poverty was measured by whether or not the father or grandfather lived with the family.

I guess the proudest thing in the neighborhood was being a part of William Penn High School's Band. As band members, we would walk through the neighborhood wearing that uniform like we knew we were somebody.

Mama would ask, "You want me to drive you to school?"

I'd say, "No ma'am, I'll walk."

It was about a twenty-twenty-five- minute walk to the school with my best friend. He played the trombone with me in the band. We'd strut through the neighborhood. We had those spats on our shoes like Michael Jackson used to wear sometimes when he danced. It gave our uniforms a little extra class. We were the first high steppers around here. Dudley High School, our main competition, went back to corps style marching under Mr. Morgan.

William Penn's Band was something special. The community started working on getting those new uniforms for the band back in 1960. They didn't get them until around the winter of 1965. I can remember the first time we wore those uniforms in the Homecoming Parade in 1966. They were the coolest things I'd ever seen.

We took pride walking through the neighborhood. As we walked, other band members would join us and we'd high step two by two. People would come out onto their porches to see us. We lived for that.

Then, another thing about the band was Concert Season. Mr. Bell, the band director, had an agreement with Mr. Ballinger who owned a clothing store. Mr. Ballinger would rent us tuxedos to wear during Concert Season. Then, we'd walk through the neighborhood wearing those tuxedos. People would walk up to us and pat us on the back saying stuff like,

"Oh, you're in the Concert Band."

"We're proud of you."

Those were proud days not just for those of us who were in the band, but it was a proud time for the whole community.

During the summertime, we all congregated at Washington Terrace Park. For a long-time during segregation, that 27-acre park was the largest park in the state where Blacks could come to get together. So, we kind of had the village concept even there. Sometimes there would be as many as twenty or thirty buses at the lower end of the park with people coming to socialize and have cookouts.

During the winter, we would go to Carl Chavis YMCA. Mr. Whitaker was the director, but everybody else up there were volunteers and they didn't take any mess. If two guys got angry with each other and wanted to fight, they'd make them put on some boxing gloves and fight man to man. Nobody ever jumped in. Even if your best friend was fighting, you were honor bound to let him fight it out man to man.

After the fight was over, they'd shake hands and there were no grudges. It wasn't like today when a whole gang of boys jump one person. Back in the day, no one would have had any respect for guys who'd do something as cowardly as that.

The Village and family dynamics might seem strange to some people, but I tell people all the time that I was very fortunate. In my life, had two real dads and two moms who gave me strength and guidance. I knew that all of them loved me. However, my Dad/Uncle will always have an honored place in my heart because it was not blood that bound us but the richness of our father-son relationship. In honor of my Dad/Uncle, after getting out of the military in 1974, I officially changed my name to Henry Wall.

Near the end of 2000, my biological father Jesse James was diagnosed with cancer. I can't help thinking of him as only a biological father because he never did the work involved in connecting with me as a son other than planting the seed. My other three brothers (his sons) and I went to D.C. to bring him back to High Point for his last days.

He lived with his only daughter throughout the last two months of his life. It was the life-long closeness that I felt for my brothers and sister on that side of the family rather than the fact that he was my biological father that influenced me to help them with him during his last days. That family closeness came from the way we did family and the way we did church as an extended family when I was growing up.

The village was just there for all of us. We were connected to the village from day one. Back then, neighborhoods throughout the South were segregated. Whether it was in the Bottoms in Kentucky, the Eastside in Dunn, North Carolina, the Eastside in High Point, or the Nocho Park Community in Greensboro some things were very much the same- home was there; family was there; school was there; and all the people who cared about us were there.

It's About the Family

Unity, Honor & Service

Elder Milton "Choo Choo" Grady

I was raised by my grandparents in Wilson, North Carolina. The first thing that they taught me, and made sure that it got in my head, was that there is a supreme being and that God is love. I learned that our primary challenge, every day, is to serve God and our brothers and sisters.

My mother was of the Methodist faith, and she was a Missionary. She loved everybody and everybody who knew her loved and respected her. My father was Baptist, but we would all go to church with Mama. Then, we'd come back and catch Daddy in the afternoon. On the third Sunday, Daddy would cook dinner for his fellowship, and we would go to church with him.

Every Sunday we would go to church somewhere. There was no choice and no excuses not to go. If you claimed to be sick, Mama would find something-boil something-get some black cough syrup or some Castor oil -make you take it, and you'd go on to church.

It was the same thing with school. Education was number two; it was very important. My grandparents only had a fifth-grade education, but they could read and write, and they took care of business. They used to preach education. We didn't miss a day of school. My greatest reward was at the end of the school year. At the end of the school year, we would get our awards, and I would come home with a grin on my face.

Grandma would say, "Let me see your report card. Let me see your grades."

And I would give her my report card for the whole year. School used to end in June back then-June 10th or June 12th. Grandma would just smile proud of the good grades, but the proudest thing would be perfect attendance. When we had perfect attendance, we used to get a certificate, and we could go to Hardee's and get a hamburger, a drink, and a shake. That was something special because Hardee's was kind of brand new back then.

Those were some of the important things about family; that I had a God in my life and that I had a father in the home. Dad was a provider. He was an educator, and he was a very loving person. He was very quiet. He didn't say much, but when he spoke everyone listened. Even his men friends' listened-cause he kept the books for his Elks Club. On his job, he was the top Black worker, because he was good at what he did. Everyone used to ask him for advice about important matters because they knew he'd think about it before he'd give an answer and make sure he knew what he was talking about.

He was a good father. He taught me how to catch. He used to play baseball in the Negro League.

I loved baseball, but we didn't have a baseball team back then. I played a lot of basketball and ran track. My best sport was swimming. I learned at the Rec Center (Recreation Center). My coach was Mr. Cox, and he taught me to swim when I was about five years old. When I got older, I used to compete against the other Rec Swim Teams around the state. That was my introduction to Greensboro, North Carolina. Back then, during the forties and fifties, Winsor Center had an Olympic size pool. It was the largest one and only one like it for Blacks in the state. All the Black Rec Centers would come to Winsor Center to compete just like it was the Olympics- all the different strokes, relay teams, diving. We did it all.

What was so unique about it was that we even did water shows. It wasn't unheard of to have enough excellent Black swimmers to perform at that level during the fifties. Everyone thinks it's brand new because you only see girls competing in synchronized swimming nowadays. Back then, we had all male teams. It was usually the biggest event of each meet with the teams having worked all year to polish their routines. There weren't any swim teams in the Black high schools where I lived in Eastern North Carolina.1 Many of the Black colleges didn't even have swim teams. So, swimming just kind of disappeared from our culture. It's a shame.

Coach Cox used to say, "Every man should know how to swim."

He had read about the plight of black men- he was a graduate of Central (North Carolina Central University), and he was determined to train up a neighborhood of champions in football, basketball, and swimming. He kept us in the water. I was a trained lifeguard at 14. He put us older boys in leadership roles all around the Rec Center.

He said, "Y'all are going to help keep everyone in line. You know the kids around here better than I do. You live with them. You go to school with them. You are the best ones to keep order around here."

It wasn't about "ratting" on each other. It was about helping to keep the place that we loved in good order. It was about helping and protecting one another. Coach Cox taught me, along with my grandparents, that I could lead people as long as I loved and respected them and they respected me.

I had that kind of teaching throughout the community. Say, one of the adults like Mrs. Jones would see me doing something wrong- She'd say, "Now Milton, you know that's not right."

We took care of one another because it was a village.

Another thing that was a part of life in the village- good food. The food was something special. It had to be right. I remember one time when the chicken didn't turn out the way my mama wanted it; she cut it up for lunch meat. Then she said, "Okay, today we'll have meat loaf." Although it was a backup meal, the flavor and care were still there. The meatloaf was just like steak; it would be so tender it could be cut with a spoon. With some carrots and string beans baked in the same pot with the juices from the meatloaf, you had a meal. I mean something good, especially with that delicious buttermilk cornbread.

No one thought about having anything else or what they might have “a taste for” other than what was put before us. There were no choices, but we didn’t mind because the food was always good. You knew it would taste good from the way it smelled while it was cooking.

I regret that I was never able to catch my grandma’s recipes. Even my oldest aunt was mad when grandma died because we couldn’t find her recipe box. All the food that we had eaten out of that house and no one could duplicate grandma’s cooking. No one could make a cobbler like Grandma. No one could flake a whole coconut for a cake like she could. Nobody could make a pound cake stand strong like she did. She was a tremendous cook. When I talk with men who grew up around the time that I did, all of them tell stories about the great cooks in their family.

Mama had one standing order in the family about gathering for Christmas Day. She would say, “Unless you are far, far away in the military or on a job far away, I want to put my eyes on you in this house on Christmas Day.”

It stayed that way with me even after I got married. I'd go to my wife's family's house the day before or earlier on Christmas Day, but by one o'clock or two o'clock, I would be at my mother's house. Sometimes my wife would say, "I don't want to go to your mother's house to cook." That was because my mother was very old school. She believed that the women in the house fed the family. As soon as we arrived, she'd say to my wife, "Put the baby down. Wash your hands and come help with the cooking." My wife came to appreciate those little cooking lessons because she eventually became one of the best cooks in the family.

Another thing about family and living in the same neighborhood was taking care of one another. Some people will try to claim that everything was good back in the day. It wasn't. Every neighborhood had a neighborhood drunk and a lady who wasn't quite a lady. In our neighborhood, Miss Lucy was both of those things.

In the wintertime when she'd be stumbling down the road drunk, my mother would bring her into the house. Mama would sober her up with a concoction that her mother had taught her to make. She'd feed Miss Lucy, help her wash up, and give her something warmer to wear. The next week, Miss Lucy would be right back out there in a ditch drunk, but Mama never stopped trying to help her.

Watching my mother dealing with Miss Lucy taught me two things: First, never judge people because you don't know what circumstances brought them to that place in their lives. And second, never give up on someone who needs help. I can't say that Miss Lucy ever got better, but I can say that my mama never gave up on her.

Another thing that my family instilled in me was a man's responsibility to the family. When I turned sixteen and was ripping and running thinking I was grown, my mother made it clear that if I messed around and got a girl pregnant that I would have to get another job. That would mean that I would have two jobs because I was going to take care of the girl and the baby. Back then, if a girl got pregnant, she had to drop out of school. They let the father stay in school because he would be responsible for taking care of the girl and the child. We already knew about responsibility by then because everyone in my family had always had chores. We knew about the care and upkeep of the house. We might not be the main cooks in our family, but we all knew enough about cooking to know how to feed ourselves.

In high school, all seniors were required to take a course called Family Life. All the classes were set up with equal numbers of boys and girls. The girls would pick the name of a guy from a hat, and that guy would be her "husband' for the year. The couple would make decisions about the family together. We'd decide whether we were going to rent or buy a home; we would budget our money; and when we learned about the different forms of discipline, we decided which form of discipline to use with our children and explained our choices to the class. We learned how to be husbands and parents. I guess that's part of the reason why most families stayed together back then.

COUNCIL OF ELDERS & JO EVANS LYNN

[1]James B. Dudley High School had a swim team that practiced and competed in the Olympic sized pool at Winsor Center until the pool was replaced with a much smaller pool around 1970.

Unconditional Love

A Lesson in Forgiveness

Elder Arthur Johnson, Jr.

I hated him. I was terrified of him. The fact that he was my father ate away at the edges of my childhood like a dog gnawing on a bone.

It was during the late 1950s and early 1960s in Charleston, South Carolina. Back then, everybody that I knew got whippings.

If you said something to one of your friends about getting a whipping, the first thing that they'd ask you was, "What did you do?"

The next question was, "What did you get

whipped with?" It was almost a point of honor to graduate from your mother's switch to your father's belt.

I didn't do anything. I just was, and it seemed that Friday through Sunday that was enough reason for my father to knock me around. A switch or a belt would have been welcomed.

He was a good father Monday through Thursday. He went to work every day. He drove a cement truck for a company. He put food on the table and clothes on my back. He took me for rides in his truck- taught me how to drive; taught me how to fish- father-son stuff like that.

But on Friday, he would go straight from work to the liquor house. Back then, some people in every neighborhood sold liquor from their houses. My father would come home drunk and mean. From the time I was about five years old, he'd pick me up, drop me to the floor and dare me to cry. Every weekend got worst and worst.

Everyone knew what was happening- not so much that what was happening to me was more than a whipping but that it lasted longer than was acceptable. It was acceptable for a mother to give a child a good whipping then pick the child up and hug the child to her breast saying, "Mama loves you. That hurt me more than it did you."

When the whipping was over, there were no hard feeling either way. The child knew why he was being punished and understood that it was a parent's responsibility to correct him. Earned punishment had been given, and hopefully, the child would not have to be punished for that infraction again.

I never knew why my father abused me.

The neighbor ladies talked about my mother because she didn't say anything or try to stop him when he knocked me around three days a week. She was young. She was only nineteen when she had me. I thought she couldn't do anything because she used to drink too and it seemed that she started drinking early enough to pass out before he got home. When she hadn't passed out, he'd hit on her too.

She was a victim of domestic violence. It seemed to be a trend with her the rest of her life. She and my father eventually got divorced, but every man she got with treated her the same way. She got married one more time but again that guy was a mean drunk too.

I was eight years old that last Saturday. I thought that maybe if I pretended to be asleep when he came back in he'd leave me alone. I heard him come in and felt him kick the mattress on the floor where I was laying.

"I know you ain't sleep, boy."

I knew that mean voice. The words were slurred together and course enough to cut. I didn't move a muscle. I squeezed my eyes shut so tight that I could see the backs of my eyelids.

"You gonna play sleep, I'll put you to sleep for good. My father turned and took his gun off of the shelf in the closet.

I was small for my age, so it didn't take much for him to roll me up in the mattress. Then he started shooting into the mattress. I remember thinking, "This isn't as bad as when he takes all except one bullet out of the gun, spends the barrel, points it right at my head and pulls the trigger."

I felt a bullet graze pass my cheek and another bullet tore off a piece of skin from my right side.

The shooting didn't draw a crowd because it was nothing for him to fire off a few shots on a Friday or Saturday night. When the gun was empty, he sat down and went to sleep. I still didn't move. I was afraid to.

"A.J., A.J. you alive?" I heard my cousin calling my name as he unwrapped the mattress.

"I guess so."

"You can't stay here. He'll kill you next time." My cousin lived in the same apartment building where I lived.

"No, he won't. I'm running away," I whispered. Sometimes my father woke up without any warning and started back up where he'd left off. "I'll go home with you."

"That won't work. My Dad's not home, and if your father comes up there and hits my mother, Dad will kill him."

I knew he was telling the truth. The last time his father and mine got into it, his Dad beat mine so bad he couldn't go to work for a whole week.

I didn't stop to pack anything. I didn't own anything worth taking. Nothing in that house had a good memory behind it. When I left the house, I wasn't sure where I was going. At least I didn't think I knew, but somehow my feet started carrying me in the direction of my grandma's house. She lived about six blocks away.

Many a weekend after that, my father, when he was drunk, would come and try to drag me back to the place where he was king. My uncles who still lived with my grandma wouldn't let him take me. I stayed with my grandma until she died when I was thirteen. Then my aunt took me in and kept me with her.

I kept that anger against my father for years. I'd see him somewhere drunk, and I'd make like I didn't know him.

That drinking finally did him in.

He was drunk one Saturday night and sitting on the rail of a second story patio. He lost his balance and fell on the cement parking lot below. He broke his neck and back. He didn't die instantly. When he regained consciousness enough to speak, he told the people at the hospital to call me.

One part of me didn't want to go- the part of me that was still that hurt, angry little boy. Another part said that it was my Christian duty to go. But it was the part of me that just barely remembered the Mondays through Thursdays when he was a good father that won out.

I went, and I took him home with me. I had to do everything for him because he was paralyzed from the neck down. I had to wash him and feed him like a baby, and when he died, I cried.

Sometimes, I think about the "good" father that alcohol took from me. I guess that's why I never took to drinking. I also learned a valuable lesson about how to love and treat my children.

When I Was Nothing but a Boy…

Lessons Learned the Hard Way

On the way from boyhood to manhood, our elders taught some of the lessons by way of a story or anecdote to drive the lessons home. Other lessons were driven home using more precise methods. I remember a story my father used a tale that went this way:

> *There was a dark forest near the village where these children lived. All their lives, the grown-ups had told them never, ever to go into the dark forest alone.*
>
> *Now, one day when the women were working in the garden planting yams and the men were hunting, some of the older boys got to feeling mannish. They dared one another to be the first one to go into the dark forest alone.*

One boy who was the closest to coming of age and leaving his mother's hut, said, "I'll go."

The rest of the boys followed him to the edge of the forest and kept watch until he disappeared among the trees.

"Don't go too deep," one of his brothers called to him. If he heard him, he didn't answer back.

The boys sat down to wait for him to return. They waited and waited until the grownups returned and they were called to dinner. The boy's mother did not know that he was missing because boys of his age began to spend more and more time with the men. She just figured that was where he was and she would see him when the women took the evening meal to the men's hut.

It was late that evening when the boys got up enough nerve to tell their elders that the boy had gone into the dark forest. His mother started to scream and cry- no one could comfort her. The boys expected the men to rush into the dark forest to save him.

But after the men asked, "Where was the sun when he went in?"

The boys answered, "At its highest point."

The men looked at one another and agreed, "It's too late."

The next morning the men went into the dark forest. They brought back an arm that looked like it had been gnarled on. The arm band that the boy's father had made for him marking his eleventh year of life proved that the arm belonged to the boy.

This story like many African stories uses fear to teach a lesson about unquestioning obedience.

Lesson: Unquestioning obedience to your elders may save your life.

******

More concrete lessons that Black men often tell about learning the hard way are told when they get together with their buddies. Some of those lessons are about the time that they got their “last whipping.” One of the elders, who shall remain nameless, tells this one:

By the time I was about 14 years old, I had figured I was too old to get a whipping. I had sense enough not to say it out loud, but I felt that at 5’11ins., I was too big for my mother, who was barely five feet tall, to take a switch to me. So, I started to ignore some of her basic rules.

They had this basketball goal near where I lived. It had four sides with goals, but we mostly used two sides for pick-up games. Only the best players among the older guys could play after about 5:00 p.m. This was when the older guys started getting off work. The rule wasn’t written down anywhere. It was just understood that you had to earn the right to ‘play with the big boys.’ I was a natural athlete so even though I was younger than most of the guys out there, I could hang with them.

The guys usually played until it got too dark to see the rim. One evening, my team was “killing” all comers. You know how it is when you are having one of those games where it seems you can't miss. Throw a ball up over your shoulder-nothing but net.

I got caught up in the game and wasn't paying attention to the fact that the streetlights had come on. Like most Moms back then, my Mom had a hard and fast rule about being in the house by the time that the streetlights came on. To save face, I usually pretended to get hurt or something so that I had a manly excuse to leave early.

Not that day. I just played on like I was a grown man.

Suddenly one of the guys yelled, "Jam Man (That was my nickname) here comes your mama with a switch."

Sure enough, she was coming through the cut (space between two buildings) carrying a switch longer than she was tall. I took off running in the opposite direction. I figured I could beat her back home and avoid getting a whipping in front of the guys.

She was so angry that I ran from her, she yelled, "Lord give me strength!"

Then she took off chasing me like she had a motor in her behind. She caught me before I'd gone 50 yards and switched me all the way home.

Lesson: Don't run. It's even more embarrassing if you get caught.

****

Parents often approach discipline differently with their male and female children. I did not learn until years later that my brothers approached gaining permission from Daddy differently than the method used by my sisters and me. Here's how one of my brothers explained it:

> *I'd wait up for him. I knew that by the time he got in from his second job, he was too tired to listen to a lot of begging and pleading like the girls would do. I'd put it to him straight- man to man.*
>
> *Like the time some boys and I were throwing rocks at the windows of vacant apartments. When the cops rolled up, the other boys ran, but I didn't. It wasn't because I wasn't scared. I stayed because*

Dad had taught us to face up when we did something wrong.

The police asked me my name and where I lived. They wanted me to tell them the names of the other boys. When we got to my house, they told Mama that if I wouldn't tell them the names of the other boys that she and Daddy would have to pay for all the damage. Mama said that she'd get it out of me. Although I got a whipping, Mama didn't wait for Daddy to get home for that, I would not tell her the names of the other boys.

She sent me to my room to wait until I could talk to Daddy the next morning before he left for work. I didn't go to sleep. I waited up until he came home. I wanted him to hear my stand about not telling on the other boys from my point of view.

I said, "Dad if those boys are my friends like they're supposed to be, they'll tell on themselves. They won't let me take the punishment for what all of us did."

He just said, "Go on to bed." He wasn't much of a talker, but I know he sided with me because Mama didn't say another word about it.

I heard later that the parents of two of the boys who were with me helped my Dad pay for the broken windows. Those two dudes and I are still friends to this day.

Lesson: Loyalty that is proven and earned is the truest bond of friendship.

What about Race?

Early Lessons in Race Relations

Elder Ezekiel Ben-Israel

I did not fully understand the impact of being a person of a different race or color until I was about twelve or thirteen years old. Growing up in a segregated society where both my parents were professionals, I'd never experienced racism on a personal level. Racism was an unspoken reality.

I saw the difference when I was in the Boy Scouts, and we went to Summer Camp. We had Black troops and White troops. When we got to the camp, immediately they started giving the leadership positions to the White Scouts. I got mad. I wasn't going to stand for that because I had always been the leader in everything, in church and school.

We would have formations every morning, raise the flag, and the bugler would be playing. I wondered how that white boy who could barely play got the job. I'd been in the band at Gillespie Junior High School. I played cornet and French horn. I was the bugler for my Boy Scout troop. It didn't make sense to me. Another thing that bothered me was the way they gave out awards. Each troop got badges for every little thing from having the most orderly camp, winning the most merit awards to placing high in certain activities. The highest scoring troop was supposed to get to fly the pennant with the Order of the Arrow.

No matter how hard we tried, every day the flag would go to a white troop. This unfair treatment kept going on until our troop leader made me the head of the troop. I came up with a strategy for winning in every activity. For example, instead of waiting for the bugle call to get up in the morning, we got up thirty minutes early. So, when the inspector came to check for made beds and such, we'd already had everything done.

We finally won the pennant, and I took over the job as bugler. Some of the White boys got mad, but there were others who came over and started jamming with us. Just about every member of my troop was in the band at Gillespie or in the band at Lincoln. We were good. The white boys who weren't mad started hanging out with us. We built a rope bridge together, we fished together, and we did aquatics together.

Now, there was a group of white boys hanging out to the side, not participating with us Black boys, but that was their thing. Although I realized that there was a racial divide, I also realized that people of both races could work together for a deeper level of harmony.

By mid-summer, something amazing was happening. When we'd come to camp, it was completely segregated. All the Blacks were on one side of the camp, and all the Whites were on the other side of the camp, but by mid-summer two of the White troops had moved their tents to the black side of the camp. I don't know why it bothered me that it was only two troops that moved. I guess even at that young age I realized that although some Whites wanted race relations to be better many more wanted things to stay the same.

I hoped for better race relationships, but still, every time a team that I was on was in any kind of competition where Whites were involved, we had to win. It was kind of like a rallying cry, "Don't lose to the white people!" It was like an unspoken reality among Blacks; never lose to white people.

I remember it. I played football at Gillespie Junior School, and when we played any of the predominately white schools like Mendenhall Junior High School and Linley Junior High School, we made sure that we beat them. In fact, we only lost one game the entire year, and that was to Lincoln Junior High School, one of the other predominately Black schools. We lost to Lincoln because we weren't prepared for an unbalanced line. It was the first time we'd ever seen an unbalanced line. We adjusted to it, but by that time the game was nearly over, and it was too late. It was the hardest game I'd ever played as the linebacker on that side. Every play, they had four or five players against me. I was kind of big for my age so I would take out one or two, but that still left two or three unaccounted for.

The next year it was the same thing. We beat all of the white teams, but we still lost to Lincoln. Most of their coaches were assistant coaches at Dudley, and they trained their players to move up to the next level. They were serious about their football. On the other hand, our coaches at Gillespie just encouraged us to have fun unless we were playing a white team.

My next taste racism was different. It was individualized racism. It happened when I went into the military. I was in the Air Force stationed in San Antonio, Texas. If you've never been there in the summer, you can't relate to how hot it is. I remember my first drill instructor; he was trying to get someone to be the dorm leader. He asked who had education beyond high school. It was me. He didn't like that. Then he asked who had been in the Boy Scouts. It was me. He didn't like that. Then he asked who was the oldest in our group. It was a white boy. He made the white boy head of our dorm. That was the first time that I felt that I was being discriminated against personally. I mean, back in Boy Scout Camp, it wasn't just me. It was all the Colored boys. I can't explain it more than that, but Black folks know what I mean.

Later on, the Drill Sargent and his closest cohort came to me and identified themselves as Ku Klux Klan members. The Sargent said, "You know we have ways of taking care of boys like you who don't know how to stay in their place."

I honestly wasn't scared. I was young, crazy, cocky and brash. I felt like I could beat the whole world.

Then one night when I was on guard duty, I turned a corner, and there was a "Colored" soldier from Louisiana hanging from a pipe about two feet off the ground. His eyes were big as the headlights on a car- like something I'd never seen before. They said he hung himself, but no one who knew him believed it. He was supposed to get married on his next leave, and he kept this big grin on his face when he showed anyone who would look a picture of his fiancée.

Next, a "Colored" soldier who worked in the motor pool had a truck he was working under collapsed on him. They didn't even investigate to find out why a man wearing his dress uniform instead of overalls was working under a truck.

I wasn't scared yet, but I was being more careful about going places alone. One day, we were having a smoke break. I didn't smoke, but I'd do about anything to escape the heat inside for a while. All of a sudden, the Sargent, was walking past me and he pushed me. The big guy who had been with him when he warned me to stay in my place, was behind me and he pinned my legs under me. It stretched my knees and my back. I went down hard. I was just lying down there on the ground hurting. I didn't say a word. But one of the other soldiers called his drill instructor, and they took me to the hospital. I had torn cartilages and ligaments in my knees, ankles and my back, contusions on my lower back, and a concussion.

I made up my mind that I was going to kill them. I didn't know how I was going to do it. But I was going to kill them. I made up my mind. I wasn't going to threaten them because I didn't want them to know I was coming. I'd never had a thought like that before- about hurting- about killing someone- but now I was in the hospital with my parents crying over me, and I wanted someone to pay for it.

Now, when you're in basic training, and you stay in the hospital out of training for so many days they will send you back to the very beginning of your training. I didn't want that to happen. So, I returned to my dorm as soon as I could. The doctor gave me some special papers to get out of some of the marching when I first came back. So, I was assigned mostly clerical duties for a while. That made the White boys even madder because they usually got all of the easy sit-down clerical jobs.

I finally figured out what the problem was. Racism went up through the ranks. The other Black guys and I kept wondering why no one ever got punished and every violent act against us was declared an accident. The officers, the NCOs, all the way up the line were in the Ku Klux Klan, and they protected the perpetrators.

In spite of it all, I made up my mind to get through Basic Training the first time around. I limped through everything that I had to do-- the drilling, the obstacle courses-everything. The Drill Sargent did everything he could to prevent me from being at the top of my class. He and the other officers took the scores that we made and ran them out to .00000 to make me number two in the class. This was too much.

The racial culture in the military was the worst racism I'd been exposed to that point, but where could I go? Who was there for me to talk to? The two men who hurt me were reassigned out of there because there had been too many witnesses to what they did.

After Basic Training, I was assigned to Wichita Falls, Texas. I have to admit that I liked it there. I met guys from all over the country. I met a guy from Winston-Salem, North Carolina and I tell you Black people from North Carolina are different from Black people anywhere else in the country. The guys from Winston-Salem and other parts of North Carolina had a more realistic view of racism. They didn't tip around the issue of racism. I think that term about "calling a spade a spade" must have originated with Black folks from North Carolina. I also found out that white folks from different parts of the country had different views of racism. For example, I met this white boy from California, and the first conversation we had was about racism in the

South. We became friends, and he was actually my roommate.

The brother from Winston Salem and I were both extroverts- loved people and loved being around people and traveling. One of the good things about being in the military is being able to travel to different places when you are off duty. We traveled together to about every town on that end of Texas. I worked in the hospital there, and racial relations were good. I didn't run into the Klan Element there.

It was different when I was stationed in Turkey. It seemed that I was the only Black person in the whole town. I ran into some real racism there, and my life was threatened. I overheard a couple of people talking, and they said that they were going to get rid of me. Immediately, my mind went back to some of the things that had happened while I was in basic training. I was scared. To make it worst, no one ever talked to me. It was as though I did not exist. I was lonely.

I ran my floor in that hospital all by myself. They would leave me written instructions for the patients about what I needed to do to prep someone for surgery or take someone downstairs for a test, but no nurse or doctor ever came up on the floor while I was up there. They would call me when there was an emergency because they wanted me to be there to assist. Otherwise, I was on the floor by myself. I received performance awards and achievement awards, but I was the only one up there. In spite of being alone, I worked every shift that I could because I was afraid to go to sleep. Every time I would doze off, I was having these dreams that my parents received a letter saying,

We're sorry to inform you that your son was killed in an accident.

Although I was getting almost no sleep, I continued to push myself. I liked to run. So, every day before I went to work, I would run along the sea wall. One day, I started out running, and something happened to me. I later found out that what I'd had was a kind of panic attack.

I remember thinking, "I have to get out of here. I have to get out of here. I have to get out of here." By the time I came to myself and realized where I was, I was at the Airforce base. All I could think about was, "How am I going to get out of here?"

It's important to understand what living there was like to appreciate how isolated I was. There wasn't a real base in that Turkish town. The Airforce rented buildings all over town as they needed them. For example, there was a building across town that they rented for the general office and another that served as the commissary about six miles away. I was living with a Turkish family.

In the meantime, I spent all my off time at the commissary. I didn't have any money. The whole nine months I was there I didn't get a single check. But they gave us a ration card, and when it was unfolded, it would reach from my waist down to the floor. The ration card was good for liquor and cigarettes. So, I started to drink and still slept as little as I possibly could.

All of the workers at the commissary were Turks, and the Turks liked Pall Mall Gold 100 Cigarettes. They'd sit and talk for a while if you handed them a couple of cigarettes. I made friends with some of them until I got written up for fraternizing with the indigenous population.

The Captain called me in. He had this Article Fifteen that he told me to sign. I refused to sign it. I never signed one of those things. In the military, signing a complaint against you is treated as an admission of guilt and can be used against you at any time. So, I never signed one of those things, but I was back to having no one to talk to.

A person can't go without sleeping but for so long. A person can go without food a lot longer than they can go without sleep. I typed up an indefinite leave slip for myself. I slipped it in with a whole stack of papers, and the C. O. signed every one of them. I packed my things walked straight to the airport. The Airport for the Airforce was just a little canopy like funeral homes use at grave sites for the family. All I knew was that I had to get out of there before someone saw me. After a while, a small plane landed. A black guy got out to unload the cargo. I went to him and told him what was going on and asked for his help.

He said, "When this plane moves, I'll leave the ladder down. You run and get aboard, and I'll get you to Ankara."

I did what he said. I got on the plane behind some boxes. When we got to Ankara, I got on the next plane by giving a guy two cartons of Pall Mall Gold 100 Cigarettes. That plane was one of those giant Cargo Carriers. It was over six stories high. I was convinced that it would not fly. I thought that maybe it was just a way to get rid of Black folks like me, but I was too desperate to be choosy. It flew though and took me to a base in Spain. From there I fell in line with a group of soldiers, and we flew to Dover, Delaware where they processed soldiers returning from foreign soil. I went and talked to the limousine driver that was headed for Washington, D.C. and told him what was going on and that I only had a dime in my pocket.

He said, “If I don’t fill up, I’ll let you aboard.”

There was one seat open. When I got to D.C., my next problem was--How do I get home? I sat in the airport for a couple of hours. I heard someone calling my name. It was a White boy from Walhalla, South Carolina. He was one of the soldiers that I had cared for in that hospital in Turkey. He had been in Vietnam, and he was messed up in more ways than I could count when he came into the hospital. In spite of what I had been going through at the time, I treated all my patients with the same level of care and dignity. It paid off because he bought me a ticket home and wouldn’t even tell me his address so I could send it back to him. He also gave me some extra spending money.

I could only get a ticket to Raleigh or Charlotte, so I chose Raleigh. I went over to a Black guy who was loading his car and told him my story.

He said, “If I have room, I’ll take you with me to Greensboro.”

He had room. I was so tired from the journey that I fell asleep as soon as I got in his car. The next thing I knew I was pulling up in front of my parent’s house.

Technically, I was AWOL (Absent without Official Leave) although I had an indefinite leave slip in my pocket. So, I went to my state senator who was L. Richardson Pryor at the time. He was a good man. He was a friend of my father. I didn't lie to him. I showed him the indefinite leave slip and told him everything about my situation. He said, "I will take care of it."

About a week later, I got a call from Pope Airforce Base. They said that if I didn't get down there within the next 24 hours, they would come and arrest me.

I said, "Arrest me for what?"

They said, "For being AWOL."

I called Congressman Pryor he said, "Go down there and turn yourself in. I've already got everything set-up."

So, I went down there to see the Officer in charge. He was so red in the face that he looked like his head was about to pop off. He started talking all this mess to me. He said that he was going to slap me in handcuffs and send my behind back to Turkey.

I looked at him and responded, "Sir you do know that I am here at the behest of my Congressman, don't you?"

He said, "I've been in the military 22 years. I'm in charge here, and I'm going to have my way with you no matter who sent you here. You go over to that building- he pointed out the window- and stay there until I send for you."

I just looked at him. He placed me on barracks arrest with an older black airman and when I saw that he only had one stripe after being in the military for over twenty years. I left him and walked all the way across the base to the Commander's office and demanded a court martial right then and there. I knew that they had heard from Congressman Pryor. So, I didn't understand what they were trying to pull.

The commander told me, "Go sit out there until we decide what to do with you. About thirty minutes later, he came out of his office and said, "Go over to the base administration office and they are going to "out" you. What you are going to get is an honorable discharge. Make sure that you read everything and if you have a problem, come back and tell me."

I went over there, and they did my physical and my psychological examination. They paid me for what by then was about 14 months. Then they handed me a package and told me to read it. I had learned from a bunch of Black guys that sometimes they put some negative codes on an honorable discharge that can prevent a soldier from finding a good job later. There were codes that mean something like "Honorable discharge under dishonorable conditions." So, I asked them to let me see the code book so that I could make sure that there were no negative codes on my discharge. There weren't any negative codes. I walked out of there with my head held high with an honorable discharge. I made up my mind that from that day forward I would make racist pay for their racism.

My Brother's Keeper

Beyond Turning the Other Cheek

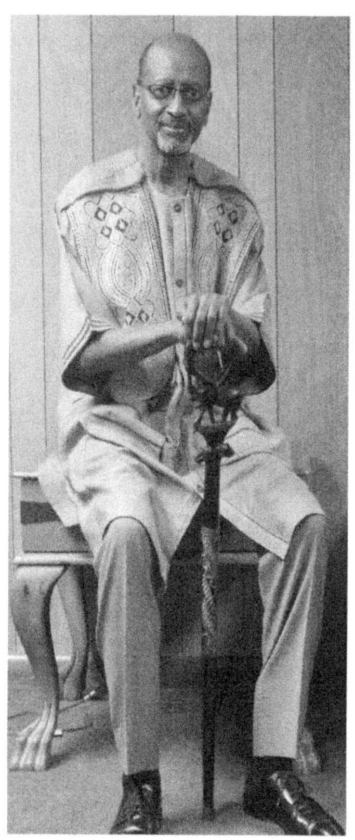

Reverend Alphonso McGlen

About twelve years ago, there was this young man who was no more than twenty, although he looked ten-twenty years older. He sold drugs. His chosen spot was on the corner of the street near the church I was pastoring in Baltimore.

Every day, he would be there by nine each morning, openly selling drugs. Since he'd been shot twice by rival gangs and survived, the people on the block seemed to think that he had “earned” the right to conduct his little business on that corner.

I guess everyone on the block was a bit afraid of him. He just looked “hard” - like he didn’t care about anyone or anything. The month that I observed him, I never saw him smile or speak to anyone other than his regular customers.

The church members said that he’d been there “forever” and since he had not approached any of the younger church members about buying drugs, the last two pastors of the church had left him alone. I made up my mind that I wasn’t going to travel that route. I would do something.

The first time I approached him, I made it clear that I just wanted to talk. I didn’t ask anything about what he was doing.

I introduced myself. I started with my youth. Telling him about having to get a job after my father died when I was twelve. I told him how everything changed after Dad died. Mom had to find a full-time job, and my older sister and I had to cook dinner and take care of the younger children. I had it in my mind that once he heard what the difficult childhood, I’d had he would understand that a difficult childhood need not determine where a person ended up in life.

Then, he told me that I was lucky to have had a father for twelve years because he'd never had one single day of knowing who his father was. He said that he'd been working since he was eight-first running numbers for the Store Lady, then being a bagboy for a big-time dealer a few blocks away.

Every day after that, we'd talk. I told him about how I'd grown up thinking that my mother's first three children were my cousins. I told him how they were being raised by her sisters in Virginia and my other four brothers and sisters lived with me.

Then, he told me that he and none of his siblings had the same father or even had a clue as to which man that their mother had been with had fathered them. He told me that he'd managed to keep his two younger brothers with him until he got sent to Juvie (Juvenile Detention) for picking up a couple of oranges from an open market for the children's breakfast. By the time he got out, they'd been placed in foster care. A couple of years ago, when they were 15 and16, he said, his younger brothers had robbed a store together and shot the owner. They'd been tried as adults and given life sentences.

He said he went to see them every other week and he seemed proud that both of them had gotten their high school diplomas while in prison.

I told him about how being a soldier had helped make me the man that I was. I'd gone into the military when I was 18 years old. It was a very disciplined, regimented, and uniformed environment. Although all the soldiers came in with different attitudes, under different conditions in life, we were trained to think and act as one. I became a platoon leader, so I had about 75 trainees who were my responsibility. They gave me a great deal of latitude to develop leadership skills that I never knew were in me. The Army has a way of stirring up and pulling out everything that is in an individual in a good way. And then, there were all the good relationships that I developed with the other soldiers. I told him that perhaps the most important thing I gained was the discipline-striving to be disciplined and the importance of having a regimen in one’s lifestyle. I wanted him to know how doing some things day in and day out worked toward physical and mental development.

Then, he looked at me and said that he had learned the same things on the Street. He told me how sometimes his mother and some of the crackheads that she hung with would stay together in an abandoned house. By the time he was nine, he was the oldest kid there. He’d take the younger ones under his wing and teach them what they needed to know to survive. He got them up and out of the house at sunup. There were dozens of government workers who’d hand a kid the uneaten part of a breakfast sandwich as they rushed to catch their train. He said that he showed the younger children how to hop a train without paying so that they could get across town to the last school that they’d attended. He said that this was important because sometimes when they changed schools, it took several weeks for the kids’ records to catch up with them so that they could get free lunches.

Then, he looked at me as though he expected me to lecture him about teaching the children how to break the law.

I kept quiet.

I'd learned by then that he had as clear an understanding of what most people saw as right and wrong as I did. He just had his own interpretation of how the rules of law applied or didn't apply to his life. He simply did what worked for him.

Once we got to know each other better, two or three times a week, we'd go to lunch together- just talking. I didn't try to preach to him. Mostly, I listened.

He said that I was the first man just to talk and listen to him. He asked me if I knew how many people walked down the street where he 'worked' every day.

I shook my head, "No."

He said it depended on the day of the week but on an average 2,346. I asked him why that mattered to him.

He said it mattered because he'd been standing on that corner off and on since he was around nine years old and not once in that time had a single man so much as spoken to him. I asked him if maybe that had to do with what he was doing at the time.

He shook his head, "No when I was younger, I was just standing there hungry because my mother didn't get food with her food stamps." He said he'd watch people in those commercials for animal shelters get all misty eyed over pictures of an abandoned dog or cat, but those same people would walk right by a hungry child.

I couldn't explain that either. I would have thought that one or more of the church members would have helped him out from time to time.

One thing I noticed, the two or three times a week that we'd go to lunch together that after lunch he did not go back to his corner to sell drugs.

He'd be there the next day though.

Another thing, I noticed about him while we talked was that he wasn't as bitter as other people I'd met who'd grown up in similar circumstances. He seemed to have made his own kind of peace with the harshness of the world. It wasn't until the second year that I began to talk to him more and more about the spiritual side of life. I think this was the hardest concept for him to connect with because he'd spent his entire life learning to depend on himself.

He was smart. He'd fallen behind in school because his mother never paid the rent. So, they moved from place to place and school to school. I think that by the end of my time at that church, he was trying to figure out why someone who'd had it so much better in life than he'd had it would need a force beyond himself to help him through life. He started to ask me questions about what I got out of what he called "that God thing."

I explained to him, as well as I could, about the joy of knowing that someone greater than you had your back. I wanted him to know that having a prayer life gave you a connection to a power whose strength made you a giant among men no matter your current circumstances.

I wasn't sure that some of what I said got through to him until a couple of years after I'd moved on to another church. I heard that he had joined the church and given his life to Christ. He was using some of the same skills that he had honed as a drug dealer to become an entrepreneur. Now, he owns several businesses, and he specializes in lifting young men out of the drug culture and bringing young women off the street to legal and gainful employment.

The Keys to Living Well

Education, Saving, and Managing Your Money

Elder Thomas Alan Bell

My Father was actually my stepfather but he was my "Dad" from the time I was eight years old. He had worked his way up to 1st lieutenant in the Army and believed that a man should be able to "pull yourself up by your bootstraps". He wasn't the type of man that sat down and discussed things with you. My family was into the adage that children should be "seen and not heard" or "don't do as I do, do as I say do".

He normally had a fulltime job and a part

time job to earn extra money. I worked with him on one of his part time jobs cleaning office buildings in center city Philadelphia when I was about 12 or 13 years old. He taught me how to do a good and thorough job when cleaning those offices. He liked for me to work with him because I learned quickly and could keep up with the workload. I had to put a percentage of everything I earned into the bank.

Little did I know that the time spent working with him would help me to earn money when I was in college. I worked part time with an office cleaning crew when I was at North Carolina A&T State University. Since I already knew how to strip, wax and buff floors, I ended up being a supervisor quickly.

Education is one of the keys to everything. There was never any doubt that I would go to college. The only question was where? My mother was a principle in the Philadelphia school system and several of my other relatives were teachers. So, it was drummed into me at an early age that education was important. I attended a high school that was 90% white and 10% black or other nationalities. That was one reason I wanted to attend a historically black college or HBCU.

The fact that I planned to major in Electrical Engineering and North Carolina A & T State University had one of the finest engineering schools in the country pretty much sealed the deal. Unfortunately, I didn't have the discipline or good study habits required to make it through the tough engineering curriculum. I ended up changing my major and earned a two-year degree in electrical technology and then a four-year Bachelor of Industrial Education degree and never left Greensboro.

When I was in high school, the focus was on the basic 3R's (reading writing & arithmetic) and on learning what we needed to know to move forward in life. No one particularly cared whether we enjoyed class as long as we mastered the material. My children were educated in the Guilford county School system and they had many more options. I know that the world has changed and that there is much more that students have to learn and understand to function in today's global economy.

The other keys to making it in life are saving (or investing) and managing your money. I remember the first time I asked for a pair of one of those "top of the line" shoe brands. My parents made it clear that if I wanted high end stuff like that, I needed a job. So, I got a paper route making $8.00 a week. Every week $2.00 went into savings at our local bank. Sometimes I didn't make the entire $8.00 because some of my customers on my paper route didn't pay their bills. Out of the total amount that I collected, the newspaper company always got their money first. Also, no matter how much money I collected, $2.00 went into my savings account, so some weeks I didn't make much for myself.

I've learned that one mistake people tend to make with their money is waiting until they have "enough to start savings". This is a big mistake because most of us seldom have enough money. The key thing that my parent's instilled in me about money while growing up was that you don't have to have a lot to get started but saving consistently over a long period of time works for almost everyone. The formula of compounding investment funds really does add up over a period of time. Some of that little $2.00 weekly savings from when I was a paperboy helped pay for college.

Another thing about managing money, you need to always pay your bills. After I turned sixteen, I had to pay to live at home. I was working. I had to pay $15.00 a week. It wasn't much now that I think about it. I could not have lived anywhere else with room and board included for that amount. But back then, I kind of resented it because my friends who were working could do pretty much anything they wanted with the money they earned.

I remember one week I didn't pay on the Friday when I got paid. Mom didn't say anything all weekend. However, that Monday when I got home from work, there were only two place settings at the table.

"Dad's not going to be home for dinner tonight?" I asked puzzling over the two plates when there were usually three of us at the table.

"Yes, he's going to be here." Mom answered without turning away from the stove.

"Oh, you've already eaten?" I asked knowing that sometimes if my mother had a PTA meeting or something at school, she'd eat early and leave the table set and food on the stove for my father and me.

"No, I'm eating, but you are not because you didn't pay me last week." She turned and looked me in the eye.

I pulled my money out and gave her the $15.00.

That taught me an important lesson. Pay your bills and meet your responsibilities on time. I later realized that principals and teachers did not make a lot of money back then and the small amount that I paid probably helped my family out a little bit. Anyway, I probably got all of it back when I went away to college.

Those lessons stayed with me. When I had children of my own, I made them get bank accounts and save some of their money. Of course, once they got older, they took it all out and spent it. The lesson did not "take" the way I hoped it would until they got a bit older and out on their own. Now all of them do a respectable job of managing their finances.

I know for a fact that if a person takes care of business – getting their education, saving on a regular basis, and managing their money that they will have better options when they get older.

The King and Queen of the House

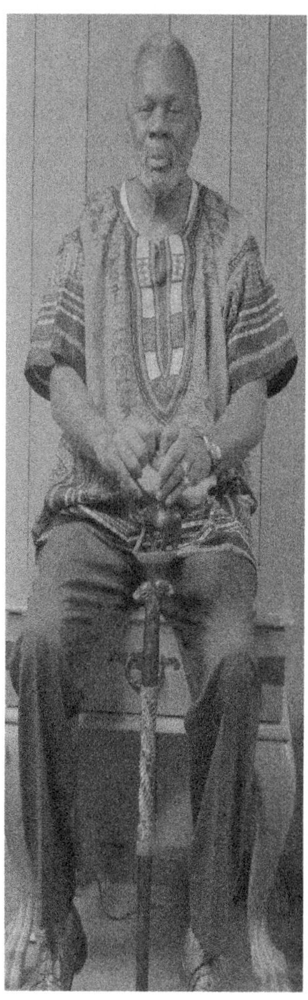

Elder John E. Wynn

In African American homes where fathers served as the head of the household, there was no question about who was in charge. Mothers made it clear that on certain issues the children had to "Ask Daddy." And fathers also made it clear that in certain areas the mother was in charge and that no matter how old a child was- 12 months to 32 years old- as long as you were living under their roof the father was king and the mother was queen.

I grew up in the Warnersville Community. It was probably the most nurturing community in the world. Everyone cared about everybody else's children. There were eleven children in my family; there were six sisters and five brothers.

We lived on the top floor of a two-story house. There's no such thing as "personal space" with that many people in one place.

Most people won't believe it, but we didn't consider ourselves poor or living in hard times. One of the joys of growing up in such a large family is learning how to love and appreciate one another. We had to learn how to get along with people, and we learned to depend on each family member to do what they could do.

Dad had to be the primary provider for the family. My mother was the guiding force in our household because my father had to work all the time. The roles of the man as the head of the household and the mother as the helpmate and primary nurturer of the children were pretty well defined when I was growing up. My father said that he knew that in some cultures women had to walk behind the men, but he told us that in our house our mother stood beside him rather than behind him.

My father's heavy workload didn't leave much time for explaining philosophical issues about life. He'd show us how to do something one time, show us one time the right way to do it, and that was it. My father was a very quiet man. He didn't say much. So, when he told us something, we knew that it was important enough to remember. By his example, he showed us the importance of work, and by his desire to take advantage of every opportunity to learn, he showed us the value of education. He had three sayings that he repeated often:

"Work for what you want; what people give you they can take away from you. You will respect and appreciate what you work for in life."

"Get as much education as you can. Once something is in your head, no one can take it from you."

"Learn something every day- a day without learning something new is a day wasted."

I learned how to treat women from my father. I guess that's the way it is with most kids-what you do as a parent is more powerful than what you say. My father treated my mother with the utmost respect. So, he taught his sons to respect women. He believed that women were God's gifts to mankind. He wanted his sons to know that the woman's place in the home was vital and that when the woman had a job outside the home, it was important for the man to rise to the level of "helpmate" around the house.

There was never any such thing as women's work or men's work in our house. Whatever needed to be done got done by the one who was available at the time. Clothes needed to be taken in off the clothesline and my sisters were busy with our younger siblings, then my brothers and I would take the clothes off the line, fold them, or iron them. All of us learned the basics of cooking. I have never understood how a man could grow to adulthood without learning how to feed himself.

My father told his sons, "The man is the head of the household, and his wife is his partner in all things having to do with the family." He knew his "place" in the family too. As the father-provider we respected his role in our family, and we valued and respected our mother's role too.

My father believed that women had more compassion and patience for raising children, so he left most of the child rearing to our mother. In spite of the clear separation of roles, we learned early in life that there was never a problem that we could not talk to either of our parents about. I never understood how important that was until I had sons of my own. I learned that if children do not feel that they can talk to their parents when they have a problem, they will just go ahead and listen to the wrong people and get into trouble.

As busy as both parents were, they found the time to build a relationship with each of their children. I know the relationship was personal to each of us because later in life when all of us children would get together each of us seemed to have different memories of what Dad and Mom were like. For example, my sisters remembered Dad as warm and loving. I never saw him that way. I knew that he loved me, but I can't remember him ever hugging me or telling me that he loved me.

The men of my Dad's generation thought to treat a son affectionately made him "soft." I never agreed with that. I guess that's why I made it a point to tell my sons that I loved them and to teach them that it was all right to show affection. I think it's a part of being compassionate and feeling empathy-being able to put yourself in someone else's shoes- helps build patience. A real man can be moved to tears. I've seen big time sports stars cry for joy after a big victory.

It seems that in those days, the family dynamics were just different than nowadays. My wife and I were very active and dedicated parents. Now, our sons are both adults that we love as our children and like as the men they have become. Both of them are educators who are kind, compassionate and concerned global citizens. Their empathy reaches beyond America to embrace mankind. They have taken the lessons of their childhood to heart. It makes me feel proud that the legacy passed to me from my parents will live on through them. They always understood what I meant when I said, "There is only one King and one Queen is this house, and that is your mother and I. One day, you will be a

King and have a Queen, but that will be in another castle."

Mastering Time Management

Relatives, Teachers, and Mentors Show the Way

Elder Larry C. Burnett

My 24-year-old father died of a heart attack when I was four years old. No one, especially my 18-year-old mother, was prepared for a young man who'd never been seriously ill in his life to suddenly die. My mother was eight months pregnant with my brother when Dad died.

She was overwhelmed after the loss of her husband.

For about a year, my brother and I lived with one relative after another relative until my grandfather, Joseph Cornelius Burnett, came and got us.

He wasn't a young man, about fifty-six, when he took us in, but he never acted like a grandfather. Our father was his son and he treated my brother and me like we were his sons. He loved his family, his community, his church, and his Masonic Lodge. He was my hero and my role model. From the time that he took my brother and me in, we had everything that we needed to be successful in life. I went off to college knowing that I was going to make it.

As a college student from a small town like Dunn, North Carolina, my freshman year of college almost did me in. I came to college at North Carolina A &T State University as one of the best and brightest of my senior class in 1976. I had been awarded a full military scholarship through the ROTC program at my high school.

Since I was the first in my family to attend college, great things were expected of me. I came in understanding the high expectations and I had a high level of confidence that I could more than meet those expectations. I wanted my grandparents to continue to be proud of me.

My grandfather was strict, but fair. Although he had only a sixth-grade education, my grandfather was a leader in the Masonic Tradition. He taught me that it was important to not only take part in an organization but it was important to also be a leader.

When I got to A&T, I was in the Army ROTC and I volunteered for the Student Advisory Board. I even volunteered at Hayes Taylor YMCA which was located near the campus. I would walk over from Scott Hall to Hayes Taylor and assist in the mentoring program. I called it volunteering but as a student on a military scholarship, I was required to complete some form of community service.

After I got involved though, I really enjoyed it. During the 25 years that I served in the military, everywhere that I went, I volunteered in the community. Mostly, I would mentor and coach basketball. I learned that coaches could be very effective mentors. Coaches, like mentors, have to meet children where they are and help them to develop to the best of their potential. Volunteering and mentoring at the **Y** was the only part of my freshman year that I never regretted or wished that I had done differently.

I went to college with good intentions and I was smart, but I kind of lost my way my freshman year because I did not have good time management. As a small-town boy coming to a city the size of Greensboro, North Carolina there was so much more to do- so many more distractions. I tried to do some of everything- volunteering in the dorm, socializing- everything.

Although I gained a great deal in the way of leadership skills in ROTC, I was stretching myself too thin. I thought because I only had class three days week, I could do what I wanted to do the other four days. I didn't understand that I needed to use those four days to prepare for my classes.

I guess part of the problem was that schoolwork had always been pretty easy for me. I'd always done my homework, but I'd never had to go beyond the basic assignments to keep up with my peers. In spite of the fact that I'd never had trouble with schoolwork before, after the first five weeks I found myself way behind. For the first time in my life, I wasn't the smartest student in every class. My mid-term reports had me failing nearly all my classes.

I had to work harder than I ever had to work in my life to catch up so that I could keep my scholarship for the next year. That meant figuring out the difference between what I wanted to do and what I needed to do. I pulled back on everything except ROTC. I needed the routine and discipline of ROTC to get myself together. It was not until my junior year that I figured out that I could do both what I wanted to do and needed to do if I managed my time wisely. One of my professors recommended keeping a personal calendar and starting every day early. Those are two things I still do to this very day.

Although I know that time management was a major issue in my near failure, I also believe that the fact that I was the first one in my family to go to college also had something to do with it. I had no one in my family as a point of reference. I had no one who could sit me down before hand and explain what college life was really like. Most good students, elementary through in high school, have parents who stay on their case about getting their assignments done. That doesn't happen in college. Parents aren't notified every time you skip a class or do not turn in an assignment. Parents need to start giving high school age children more responsibility for their own success.

I did not have problems in college because I did not have tremendous teachers and mentors along the way. My Sunday school teacher, Mr. C.C. Ray, made sure I had a good spiritual foundation, and my teachers Mrs. Veronica Surles and Mrs. Leonard Arnold made sure that I was ready academically. There were also men in my life other than my grandfather, like Donnie Olds, Dr. Pete Brewington and Coach Jim Toon who served as mentors. I have a say that the Army ROTC at North Carolina A&T State University with men like Lieutenant Colonel Lazell Free and my career in the military with women like General Clara Adams-Ender helped mold me into the man I am today.

My commitment to helping others is driven by my relationship with my grandfather, my teachers, and my mentors.

Lessons Well Learned

Elder McArthur Davis

I grew up in a single-parent household with three siblings- a sister five years older, a brother three and a half years older, and a brother one year and a half years younger than me.

My Mom worked as a domestic for a wealthy white family for the majority of my childhood. Money was always very tight. However, she made sure my siblings, and I always had life's essentials (food, clothes, and shelter). We also had all of her love. I know now that love was the most important thing in life she could provide.

My mother was a classic, hopeless romantic and due to her optimistic outlook on relationships and marriage, she was married and divorced twice before I was twelve. Like most children of divorced parents, I was not completely sure of the reasons for the divorces. However, I think that the way she talked to the men in her life had something to do with it. Even though she was only 5'2 inches tall and weighed less than one hundred fifteen pounds, she was very outspoken and strong-willed and would not quietly accept her mate's bad behavior.

Needless to say, due to my mother's relationships or lack of stable relationships, I grew up during the early part of my childhood without a strong male figure in my life that I could look up to and respect. That all changed when I was around thirteen yours old, this guy started coming to visit my Mom.

I remember thinking even then, that he had no chance of surviving in a relationship with my Mom. She was a little lady who only had an eighth-grade education, but she also had a high intellect and verbal skills that far exceeded her educational level. This intimidated most men. I expected it to be the same with Lee even though he was a big guy- maybe 6'2 and over 200 pounds. I just knew that he stood no chance. She would dismantle him. To my surprise, they were together for over thirty years. They never married, but they were together.

Lee was the only adult male in my life that I respected because he looked out for me. He taught me how to drive, and he was kind and gentle with my mother. She could get loud and be a handful. But I never heard him raise his voice or saw him raise a hand to hit her. The only way that we'd know that he was upset was he would become quiet or leave the house for a while.

I remember one time when I was about 13, I got into a fight with a kid in the neighborhood, and the kid's mother came out of their house and started fussing at me.

I started cussing at her. Throwing out every cuss word I could come up with like I was grown. Then, the boy's mother's boyfriend came out and grabbed me up by the back of my shirt.

Right then, Lee pulled up in his car and said, "Put my son down."

Lee was a kind of big guy. The man put me down and backed away.

Lee put me in his car and all the way home I was laughing and bragging, "I won that fight. I beat his a%$$###.

He didn't say anything until we pulled up in front of the house.

Then he turned to me, and he said, "I've never been so ashamed of anyone in my life. You didn't win anything."

"I won that fight," I said. I thought maybe Lee had missed the fact that I had won because he arrived after the actual fight had ended.

"No, you didn't. You lost something even more important. You lost your head. Those people heard you ranting, cussing, and raving like a mad man. You lost the respect of everyone there because you allowed someone to push you to the point that you lost respect for yourself by using language like that. You lost that fight."

He didn't say anything else. He just got out of the car and walked into the house. As far as I know, he didn't say anything about the fight to my mother either.

From that day forward, I never used another cuss word. I learned that I could tell someone off without cussing them out. In fact, I have found that it confuses an opponent when you remain calm and articulate while they are ranting and raving.

Be Ready! Be Ready!

"The One that Reads Leads"

Elder James Aquilla Smith

I was raised in a small-town east of Greensboro. I know a lot of men my age have stories about coming up with a hard life. I don't. My childhood was perfect. Both parents were there, and both were very much involved in my life and education.

I can't say I never got a spanking, but I know that I was never abused. We didn't have a lot, but we had everything that we needed.

My mother worked in the school's cafeteria. So, I couldn't get away with very much. All it took was for the teacher to go to the cafeteria and tell my mother that I was out of order and I was in trouble. I knew that if my mother had to stop cooking to come and see about me, it would not be a good thing for me. I knew that I'd get a spanking or even worse.

Back then, it didn't take a whipping every time to straighten a child out. My mother could just give me "that look" that said that she was disappointed in me and it was worse than a whipping.

Besides my parents, another mainstay in my childhood was going to church. There were no "ifs" "ands" or "buts" about it. Every Sunday we'd be in church. By the time I was in elementary school, my church attendance was so regular that I was teaching a Sunday school class of four and five-year-olds. It wasn't that I was all that spectacular as a teacher. It was just that they could depend on me to be there every Sunday. Being a Sunday school teacher was my first leadership role. When I got to high school, my next leadership role was as captain of the basketball team.

Although my father only had a fourth-grade education, he stressed the importance of education to us kids. He explained that although he was skilled at what he did in the furniture factory, he could not move up as far as he should have because other men with more education kept moving up ahead of him.

He always said, "The one that reads leads."

And he said, "The one who is ready works steady."

Those sayings kind of stuck with me. I was interested in auto mechanics and SCCA (Sports Car Club of America). There are all kinds of books about both subjects. When I read a story about someone's life, I paid special attention to the mistakes that they had made and what they'd learned from their mistakes. If a person can learn from the mistakes of others, it will make their life a lot easier.

It bothers me that young people today don't seem to spend very much time reading the kinds of material that will help them move forward in life. I have been involved in several mentoring programs. In 1988, I founded a program in Rockingham County called Youth for

Truth. The program focused on reading and getting ready to have the best future possible. The only people who don't have to read to get ahead are those who are "born to money." The rest of us, no matter which race, have to read to succeed.

We also have to prepare ourselves. I had a gift for working with cars, but that gift would not have done me any good if I had not studied and kept up with the changes in automotive engineering and design. I guess everyone knows someone who had a natural gift for something but never got anywhere with that gift. It is easy to blame that failure on others, or in tragic circumstances, but most of the time the failure is on us if we don't do the work that it takes to make our dreams come true.

My parents did not have a lot of money to give me, but they did give me the knowledge of the importance of education, God, and a strong work ethic. I used it all, but I think that the reading helped the most to move me forward in life.

Any and everything you need to know can be found in a book somewhere. During slavery time, Black people weren't allowed to learn how to read because the slaveholders knew how powerful reading and knowledge could be.

I found that knowledge and being good at whatever you do is the best way to overcome racial issues. In SCCA, the racing crews are almost always all white. But, in that industry, the wealthy car owners only care about one thing-WINNING. I was naturally good with my hands, and I read and kept up with all the ways to make cars go faster. The fastest car wins. A man who can make sure that their car is the fastest and that their crew performs like a well-oiled machine during every pit-stop can become an SCCA Crew Chief no matter his race. I'm living proof of that. I was a Crew Chief at a time when everyone on the crew except me was white. A Crew Chief has to be a good leader, and I had started training for that back when I started teaching Sunday school.

A Crew Chief has to be better than just "good." A Crew Chief has to be able to take a car apart and put in back together in a matter of hours. Perhaps, the most important aspect of being a crew chief is that the head of a crew has to know how to do everything that needs to be done. When I first started out, they would throw all kinds of small jobs at me. I didn't complain. I took each task as an opportunity to learn. I got good at everything, and it wasn't long before I could complete each task faster and better than anyone.

There came a time when during a pit-stop, I'd have my tire changed and would be standing there waiting for the other three guys to finish. Eventually, the guys respected the fact that I knew what I was doing and that I was better at it than anyone else who was doing it at the time. That level of respect was necessary because a Crew Chief has to be able to take the input about how the car is operating from the drivers- whether the car is pulling a certain way- it's not accelerating right- whatever- and make the changes needed to make the car go faster. The ability to lead and to make a car go faster was the top priority.

I remember one time when the car owners, two white men, flew me up to Portland Oregon to head a racing crew. They picked me up at the airport and took me to a Steakhouse to meet the other 20-25 members of the crew. Talk about *Guess Who's Coming to Dinner*; I was the only Black person in the place. All the rest of the crew knew about me was my name, James Aquila Smith. Naturally, they were taken aback that the owners would bring in this Black man from North Carolina to be their crew chief.

During the meal, they kept throwing out all these questions at me. But, because I'd read and kept up with all the specifications and knew what I needed to know, I could answer all of their questions. The proof of my ability came during the next few days preparing the car to meet specifications and to run better and faster than any of the other cars. Once the crew saw the quality of my skill, I didn't have any trouble leading that crew.

I was glad that I was ready when those White men gave me the opportunity to head crew. But I must admit that given the racial climatic of the time I was a little nervous about traveling to all those places like Portland, Oregon, Atlanta, Georgia, Sebring, Florida, and Canada as the only Black man among dozens of whites.

When I talked to my father about my concerns, he said, "They have the same God in those places that we worship. Just say your prayers every night and do the best job you can do. God's got you."

I always did that and although sometimes people would say or do little things. Nothing was done to me physically that I could not handle. Now, when I work with the Electric Car Team at James B. Dudley High School, these are the lessons that I stress education through reading, being prepared by learning and perfecting your craft, and faith in God as your protector and guiding power.

Mighty Men Move Others to Greatness

Elder Robert Purvis

Golden Frinks was the driving force in my connection to the Civil Rights Movement and Black History. During the early sixties, in Williamson, North Carolina, I was his personal driver. I learned a great deal about myself and my place in the world by being around a man like him. I learned how to do for myself and to respect myself as a Black man.

Being around a man like Golden Frinks, who was

putting his life on the line every day for others, moved me to fulfill my destiny. He was willing to go anywhere to help move Civil Rights along. Many a night when we would get in too late for me to drive home, I slept in his daughter Goldie's bed because she was away at school.

We traveled everywhere. I participated in the first March on Washington, but as a young man what impressed me the most at the time was getting to meet all of the celebrities like Harry Bellefonte and big names in the Movement like Dr. Martin Luther King. I didn't understand the full impact of the March and Dr. Martin Luther King's speech until later on when I looked at it through the prism of Civil Rights history.

I knew a great deal about Black History from my Senior Black History Class in high school. Back in 1962, before integration, Black History was a required course for all seniors. My Black History teacher, Mr. Fred Bennett, told me, "In this state, you're required to study North Carolina History, United States History and World History. It does not make sense for you not to know your history. He did a thorough job of teaching us about the people and events that weren't typically found in the history books adopted for high schools in North Carolina in those days. Mr. Bennett went beyond the history book to stress the importance of education, a college education, and hard work.

But it was my graduation that drove the lessons about Black History home. My principal, who was Mr. W.A. Holmes had a classmate at Morehouse College, Dr. Benjamin E. Mays. Mr. Holmes invited Dr. Mays to be our commencement speaker. Because I had taken Black History, I knew who Dr. Mays was. He was not only the president of Morehouse College; he was a mentor and advisor to Dr. Martin Luther King, Jr. In fact, Dr. King often noted that Dr. Mays' theories on racial relationships, later documented in the book, *Born to Rebel,* that laid the foundation for Dr. King's strategy for achieving civil rights for Blacks.

In my Black History class, we were required to learn one of Mays' most famous quotes, the one that no doubt served as inspiration for Dr. Martin Luther King's "I have a dream speech." Years before Kings' speech, Dr. Mays said,

> *"It must be borne in mind that the tragedy of life doesn't lie in not reaching your goal. The tragedy lies in having no goal to reach. It isn't a calamity to die with dreams unfulfilled, but it is a calamity not to dream. It is not a disaster to be unable to capture your ideal, but it is a disaster to have no ideal to capture. It is not a disgrace not to reach the stars, but it is a disgrace to have no stars to reach for. Not failure, but low aim is sin."* Benjamin Elijah Mays

So, I knew who Dr. Benjamin Mays was. The very idea that someone of his stature who was in the history book that we had studied; someone who was still alive in 1962 would come to our graduation. It was amazing that someone like that thought enough of our principal to come and speak to a small class of 100 seniors in Williamson, North Carolina (A town of fewer than 5,000 people). It was mind boggling. For years afterward, Dr. Mays' words were like a drumbeat to my social consciousness.

I also got to attend the first meeting of the Southern Christen Leadership Conference at

Virginia Union University. I met Stokely Carmichael and other men who were leaders in that part of the Movement. During that time, I had many opportunities to participate in protest marches and other aspects of the Civil Rights Movement. It was a time when I was able to define myself as a man.

It had a great deal to do with being around strong people who were making great sacrifices every day. Their lives were in danger every minute of every day, but they never put their lives ahead of the Movement. A person can't be around people who are that strong and passionate about making a difference and not be moved to do his share.

We had most of our meetings in a church in Williamson, North Carolina called Green Memorial Church of Christ. That was the church where we rushed to keep from being arrested or water hosed. I got arrested so many times during those protests that I finally migrated to Boston, Massachusetts which was our Sister City at the time. The city kind of adopted those of us who had participated in the Movement. So, many of us relocated up North to Boston and other cities.

Now, another person who was important in my development to manhood was my father. One of the most important lessons he taught me was about my responsibility as a member of a family. It happened this way,

> One of my friends told me, "My mother gives me an allowance."
>
> "What's an allowance?" I said puzzling over this new term.
>
> "It's money she pays be for emptying the trash, mowing the lawn, raking the yard, and cleaning my room. Stuff like that."
>
> "You mean you get paid for raking the yard, taking the trash out and cleaning up after yourself?" I could not get a handle on someone being paid for doing the things that I did and didn't get a penny. Frankly, I thought he was lying until he pulled five dollars out of his pocket.
>
> The other two boys who were with us, Mike, and Thomas, said that they got allowances too. At first, I wasn't mad about it but the more I thought about it, the more worked up I became.

I kept thinking about it until my father got in from work. I decided to ask him about it. I thought that maybe he didn't know that he was supposed to give me an allowance.

I told him, "Dad, Dennis and some of the other guys say that they get an allowance for all the things they do around the house."

He looked at me and said, "And?" Just the one word like he didn't understand what Dennis and the other guys getting money had to do with me.

I explained, "Dennis and the other boys do the same things that I do around here, but they get paid for it."

My dad thought about it for about ten seconds then he said, "I'm never going to pay a child to live with me." Then he just walked away like he'd said everything that he had to say.

I figured out what he meant. He worked. My Mom worked and cooked and cleaned. Every member of the family had jobs that they were responsible for doing. Taking out the trash, raking the yard, and picking up after myself were my contributions as a member of the family.

That lesson and the other boyhood lessons, the lessons about Black History, and all that I learned during the Civil Rights Movement stuck with me. Throughout the many years that I worked with the Boy Scouts of America, I made those lessons about understanding my place in the world as a man and my responsibilities as a member of a family the mantra of all that I did.

Family, God, and Country

A Brother and a Friend

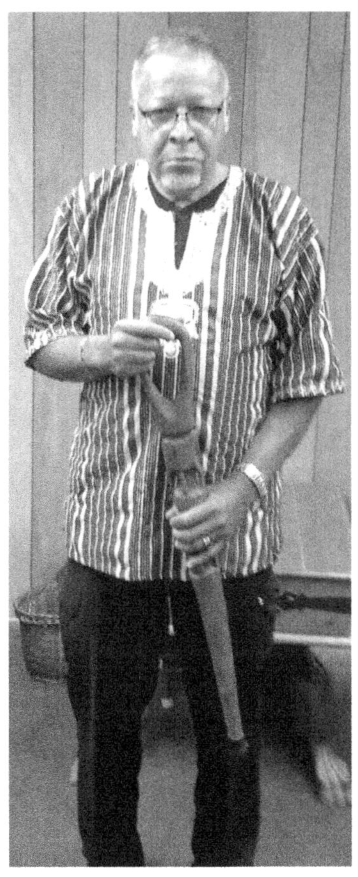

Lt. Col. C. Girard Johnson

If you live long enough, there will be dark days. Some of those dark days will be of your own making and others will come down on you so hard and so fast that you feel as though heaven and hell are caving in on you at the same time. Some of the darkest days of my young adult life were of my own making.

I had graduated from James B. Dudley High School in 1969 and was a freshman at North Carolina A&T State University. Since my family lived in Greensboro, my parents saw no reason for me to live on campus.

My father had always had a very strict set of what he called his "House Rules." I was a grown man-18 years old. None of my new friends had curfews. Anyway, parties didn't really get started until after 10:00p.m. It didn't make sense to me that a grown man- a college man- should have the same curfew that he'd had in high school.

The first night I stayed out late, my Dad was waiting up for me.

He said, "Did you forget that this is my house and my rules?"

"I said, "No, sir." And when he didn't say anything else, I went on to bed.

The next time, all he said was, "My house. My rules."

The third time I came home late, my clothes were packed up on the front porch. The house was dark and for the first time the doors were locked. None of us kids had ever needed keys because my mother did not work outside the home and at night we were required to be in before my Dad locked the doors before going to bed. I gathered my clothes and went to spend the rest of that night on the floor in a friend's room in Scott Hall.

I waited until I knew that my Dad would be home from work the next day before going to talk to my parents. I knew that even if my mother wanted me to come back, she would not go against Dad's wishes. When Dad got home, I asked him why he'd put me out without warning.

He said, "I told you twice. My house. My Rules. Any child of mine who's too grown to follow my rules can't live here."

I think he wanted me to promise that I would never stay out late again and beg him to take me back. I didn't say a word.

I went and found a friend who didn't like staying on campus and we rented an apartment together. I had to get two more jobs to cover my share of the bills and buy food. I say two more jobs because I already had a work-study job on campus working in the cafeteria. Having to work two additional jobs while going to college sucked almost all the fun out of college. I wasn't all that big on having fun anyway. Two of the nights that I'd stayed out late I was in Scott Hall swapping tales with a couple of guys. I wasn't really a party person.

Anyway, I had a very solid reason for wanting to do well in college. One of my teachers at Dudley had said, "Clifton, you are never going to amount to anything because you have a bad attitude. You'll probably end up on the street." I made up my mind that day that I would graduate from college and go back and wave my diploma in her face. So, I worked three jobs so that I could stay on my own and make my own "house rules." I graduated in 1974 with a degree in engineering and entered the United States Air Force as a commissioned officer.

****

August 10, 1992, was one of those dark days that hit my body and spirit so hard that I couldn't see an end to the hurt. That was the day that my brother and best friend Lt. Col. Wendell "Sheik" Johnson died. Even after I left home, we were as close as we'd ever been. Every kid who grows up in a home as strict and structured as ours needs a friend. You know what I mean, someone you can complain and let off steam to without worrying that what you say will go any further. Someone who will take your side right or wrong, but let you know, without dressing it up, when you are wrong. Wendell was that someone for me - a friend and brother.

Growing up with Wendell was a grounding force in my life. We grew up in the Dudley Heights section of Greensboro, North Carolina on Ross Court. It was a very close-knit community of strong, middle class, working families. Our parents were very much involved in our education at Bluford Elementary, Lincoln Junior High School and James B. Dudley High School. We attended Grace Lutheran Church and the community, schools and church added even more structure to what our parents gave us at home.

My parents still live in the same house that we grew up in and my brother Wendell planned every family Reunion to coincide with his three weeks of leave. I cannot put into words how much that "home place" means to me now. I understand now that it was more than just a place of "house rules"- it was, and still is, about family. It is about making the kinds of shared memories that help you get through those dark, dark days when the ones you shared them with are gone.

At family get-togethers we talk about how Wendell would always be the one to step in and stop any disagreements before fists started to fly. We laugh about how we would tease him about the time when he was five and climbed behind the wheel of Dad's car, released the brake, and rolled the car down a hill and into a tree. We smile knowing that if that had been any of us kids other than Wendell, we probably would not have made it to our next birthday. We speak quietly when we remember how he was so much into every activity at Grace Lutheran Church that our parents were convinced that he was going into the ministry.

No family gathering is complete until each of us reminisces about the many small acts of kindness Wendell was known for doing without being asked. We talk about how he was always willing to help out-doing more than his share of any task. Then we get quiet remembering that it was his willingness to work, although he was technically still on leave that led to his death. You see, he went to work on August 10, 1992, on a practice flight in place of the scheduled systems officer who called out because of a family emergency. Yes, there are some memories that all of us- his family, his friends, his co-workers share, but there are some that only Wendell and I shared.

I suppose that among siblings there are always differences in the way “blood’ connects. There were six of us, but Wendell was special in different ways to each of us. Wendell and I were each other’s best friend. Neither of us ever made a major decision without running it by the other one. We shared a love of model planes and ROTC. We joined the Air Force together and stayed in as Career Men (Wendell 19 years and me 25 years). We made the rank of lieutenant colonel on the same day. We both loved our job assignments in the military. Wendell was a commander of academics at the fighter weapons school- the operations officer of the 57th Wing’s F-15E Division at Nellis Air Force Base in Nevada. I was a systems inspector whose job required me to travel to military bases all over the world. Although I was only home thirty days a year, Wendell and I remained close.

There is a certain camaraderie among men in the military. It comes with the structure and tight discipline. It's there in the preparation for duty. It is bread in the loyalty to our country and the trust that in times of danger we have each other's back.

Wendell and I had all that long before we joined the military.

Creating Leaders

Connecting with My Culture

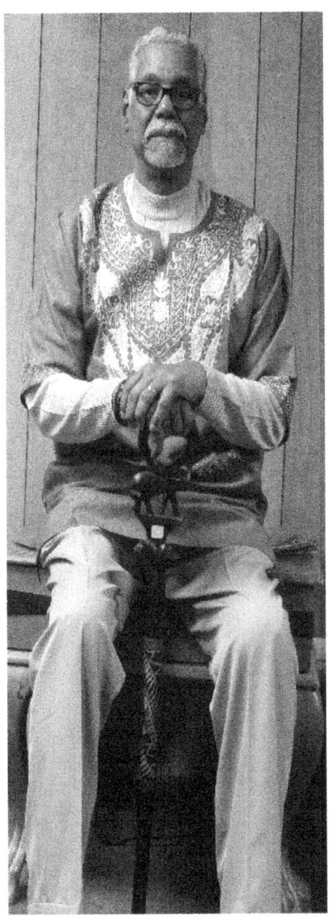

Elder Ralph D. Mitchell

I grew up in a loud household with nine children in Madison, Wisconsin. As the fifth child, I was right in the middle. A middle child has to find their own place of leadership because in all probability they will never be the first one in the family to do anything.

People often ask how my family ended up in Madison, Wisconsin. Actually, my siblings and I were the third generation to live there.

My maternal grandparents, William, and Anna Mae Miller

were part of the first Negro Colony of Freedmen who migrated north to less hostile racial environments after the Civil War. They owned the first home purchased by blacks in the 600 block of East Dayton Street.

William Miller attended law school and worked for Governor Robert Lafollette. Anna Mae was a college-educated teacher. Their home became a gathering place for early literary, political, and civil rights meetings. My grandfather helped build the community's first black church, St. Paul African Methodist Episcopal Church. Radical Black scholar W.E.B. DuBois stayed at their home several times during speaking engagements in Madison.

My grandfather named one of his sons after DuBois and my parents followed that tradition with my middle name. My mother said that she and her siblings did not have to deal with some of the types of overt racism that most blacks had to deal with in other parts of the country. I guess it was because there were so few Blacks in Madison and because my mother and her siblings were very fair skinned, with straight hair. They probably "fit in" with the other kids in the community. However, because my father looked as though he'd just gotten off the boat from Africa, strong, dark, handsome Negroid features, my siblings and I were varying shades of brown that left no doubt that we were Black.

My Father's name was Ernest "K P" Mitchell. He was born in 1913 in Sherard, Mississippi. Sherard was a rural community made up of mostly sharecropping families.

Definition of sharecropper: a tenant farmer especially in the southern U.S. who is provided with credit for seed, tools, living quarters and food, who works the land and who receives an agreed share of the value of the crop minus charges.

In Mississippi and other Southern states, sharecropping was a way of keeping slavery alive. Since most of the former slaves could not read or write and the landowners kept track of the "credits." Every year the sharecroppers ended up owing money rather than making money from their labor. This debt bound the sharecroppers to the land because there were laws that required the repayment of all credit before leaving.

The housing for sharecroppers wasn't much better than the living quarters had been for slaves. My father spent the first 13 years of his life in a one-room shack with a dirt floor with his parents, siblings, and a couple of his mother's sisters. My Father was the cause of my Grandfather gathering his family and fleeing Sherard, Mississippi in the middle of the night. This is the story that I was told:

> *Ernest and his brothers along with some other black boys loved baseball and played whenever they got the chance to get away from their responsibilities in the sharecropping fields. The landowner's son and the sons of some of the poorer white farmers played baseball with them. However, the owner's son was not that good.*
>
> *They let the owner's son play though because he owned the only baseball, a couple of bats, and a glove. Without his equipment, the black boys had to make do with a whittled stick and a rag ball. So, when sides were chosen the white boy was always picked first and his team was usually made up of the rest of the white boys. His side always won because he was*

spoiled and had white privilege on his side and he knew it.

This went on for a while. The white boys' team won, and the Black boys capitulated to his wishes just like their parents did with his parents. By 1927, there were strict segregation laws in place.

When Ernest was about 14, he decided that he'd had enough of that mess. It didn't make sense to him that the white boy who wasn't nearly as good as the worst Black player on Ernest's team always had to win.

That day, there were no slow pitches every time the owner's son came up to bat. He struck out three times. Instead of making sure that every hit ball went to center field or left field, the boys hit fly balls to right field where the owner's boy always played. Of course, he never caught a single ball.

The owner's son was furious. After winning for so long, he figured that there was no way he could lose in a fair game. He accused Ernest's team of cheating.

> *Ernest said, "We didn't have to cheat. We beat you fair and square."*
>
> *The owner's boy pushed Ernest and slapped him. He thought he could get away with it because he was white. Ernest was ready and more than willing to fight. He whipped that white boy, up one side of the field and down the other side. Ernest didn't get any formal training in boxing until later, but people say that even at 14 he had fists like sledgehammers.*
>
> *Later that night, after midnight, a white farmer came to my grandfather's shack and told my grandfather, "A bunch of white men is coming to get Ernest and your other boys. It doesn't look good for their lives. Right now, they're working themselves up with liquor. You folks should get out of the state right now!"*
>
> So, *Ernest's family packed everything they could carry and started their journey north, eventually ending up in Madison, Wisconsin.*

And that is how my father's family ended up in Madison, Wisconsin.

My Father was a quiet man. His family was completely different from my mom's family. Folks say that opposites attract and in the case of my parents this was certainly true. Dad was an introvert and Mom was an extrovert; her whole family was extroverts. He was dark skinned she was light skinned; her whole family was. The Miller's saw themselves as a part of the talented tenth. They were elitist. Grandfather Miller was trained as a lawyer and his wife as a teacher. That was quite an accomplishment, less than fifty years after slavery ended.

My mother and her siblings enjoyed a very fine, high quality of life. They had a cook and a nanny and lived very privileged lives until the death of their father. St. Paul AME Church was mostly light skin people. My grandmother Miller formed a book club made up of the black intellectuals in Madison at the time. Many were in Madison going to grad school at the University of Wisconsin.

My grandmother could not understand why her daughter, my mother, would want to be with such a darker skin person. Grandfather Miller did everything in his power to keep my mother and father apart including sending my mother miles away to their summer home. That did not work because my Dad was determined and in love. It was too far to walk. He did not own a car, but he got to where my mother was any way.

My grandmother Miller and my father never had any relationship. She didn't speak to him. However, since her daughter's children were her blood, she poured a lot of black history into us and told us we were special and were not to act like those other uneducated Negroes on the other side of Madison. I believe that my grandparents on the Miller side were ashamed of being black, but because the fact that they had light skin did not matter to some whites they became brave civil rights fighters.

My father's side of the family, the Mitchell side, overcame almost all of the worst residual effects of slavery and its aftermath of unbelievable poverty. My Father was a football star in high school. He was also city and conference heavy-weight boxing champion. He accepted a scholarship to play football at the University of Toledo in 1933. Shortly after he got to the University of Toledo, he received a letter that my mother was pregnant. He came home got married and started an apprenticeship to become a chef at the University of Wisconsin. He became a chef and cooked for the University until he retired just before his death in 1970. He was 56 years old.

My dad worked a total of three jobs for as long as I can remember. He always had places where he would do janitorial services. I would get up at 2 a.m. seven days a week to work with my dad. I started when I was five years old. My older brothers worked with him too, but as soon as they could find another job, they left me alone with dad. I worked with him until I went off to college. By working with him, I spent more time with my dad than any of my eight siblings.

While we worked, my father talked to me about the importance of family. He told me, "A man should be willing to 'die' for his wife and children. A man must do whatever it takes to feed his family and put a roof over their heads."

He looked me in the eye and said, "Ralph, you have to promise me that you will bring your family up with more than I provided for you."

I said, "I'll try."

He said, “No, you will, or you will die trying. I promised my father the same thing that I am asking of you. I was born in a shack. Haven’t I done better than that for you?”

I nodded, “Yes.”

“Then how can you be satisfied saying that all you’ll do is try?”

He wasn’t satisfied until I promised to do better for my family than he had done for his family.

It wasn’t that he had not done a good job with his family; we lived in a decent house, and we got an excellent education in the Madison Public Schools. We didn’t have to deal with a lot of racial issues like segregation simply because my siblings and I were usually the only African Americans in the schools. I didn’t realize until later on that the class system among the Blacks in Madison was based more on how wealthy a person’s employer was than on the color of their skin.

My father was a proud man, and all his children went to college. However, long before I got to college, I learned the value of hard work and how to do things the right way the first time.

When I first started working with my dad, I had to do so many of my chores over and over until I got them right. I learned that doing things right is a matter of focus.

Dad would say, “If you are doing something, doing it right should be the only thing on your mind until it’s done.”

He also said that there was no excuse for me not to provide the opportunity for my children to get the best education they could get. He made me promise that I would make sure that my children went to college.

He said, “Don’t let them do like I did.”

I am proud of both sides of my family, but I did not understand how much I was missing by not having a true connection to my culture until I went away to college. In 1961, Knoxville College was like other Historically Black Colleges at that time. I was introduced to Blacks from all over the country. I cannot describe the richness of that experience and what it has meant to my life.

I joined a fraternity, Omega Psi Phi, and it was one of the most powerful leadership experiences of my life. Back then, the Greeks ruled the campuses. We were the top athletes, and we had the best grades. In college, being at the top of your class academically means a great deal. Greeks held every office on campus. We were the core of the academic and social life of the campus. We were the leaders.

While I was in college, my summer job was working as a dining car waiter on the Great Northern Railroad traveling from Chicago to Seattle, WA, home based in St. Paul, Minnesota. As a waiter, I met people from all over the Northwest and Midwest as well as those from the east coast. People from all over the country were traveling to go to the World's Fair in Seattle. Doing what some would call menial labor taught me some essential leadership skills about listening and thinking before speaking.

There are several myths about leadership that has kept people without the knowledge from wanting to be leaders. I have made it my life's work to dispel those myths.

1. Leadership is a rare skill. *All of us have some ability in the Leadership arena.*
2. Leaders are born, not made. *Leadership is learned through experience.*

3. Leaders are charismatic. *We all have charisma. It depends on the situation.*
4. Leadership exists only at the top of an organization. *It exists all through the organization as well as a family.*
5. Leaders prod, push, control and manipulate. *Leadership's primary purpose is to enable, empower, and energize others.*

My parents made it a point to expose their children to a broad range of leadership building experiences. I was a Cub Scout, a Boy Scout, and I played three sports. In 1961, I accepted a basketball scholarship to Knoxville College, Knoxville, Tennessee. I graduated in 1966. I got drafted six months later. I qualified for Officer Candidate School in the United States Army

Being in the military was one of the most important leadership building activities of my life. There was such a wealth of new experiences in the different places where I was stationed that I could not have enjoyed myself more. I was in the infantry, and I spent most of my time in Europe with a NATO Unit. There were many opportunities to develop leadership skills, and I tried to take advantage of every opportunity to continue to develop my leadership skills.

After the military, I worked at a youth center in Princeton, New Jersey for about a year. My oldest brother worked in New Brunswick, New Jersey. He was a Dean at Rutgers University. I commuted from his home to the Princeton Youth Center. My brother decided that he wanted to work for a Historically Black Institution. So, I went with him to Durham, North Carolina to have a look at some of the colleges in the area. He ended up working for Shaw University.

While there on that visit, we went to a house pool party and I was offered a job working with Manpower Development Corporation which eventually changed its name to MDC, Inc. I worked for them for a few years until I married my wife in her hometown of New Haven Connecticut. When I met my wife, she was one of my brother's students.

While in New Haven, my wife and I joined The Nation of Islam. It was never a spiritual thing for us. It was about, how can we help black folks? We knew that we as a people were in deep trouble. For me, the main thing that came out of that period of my life were the teachings about Black ownership, independence, and entrepreneurship. At the time, we thought The Nation had the answers.

I believe that once someone is as thoroughly steeped in Christianity as we both were in childhood with meaningful examples in our lives of true Christianity, it's hard to convert to another faith. For my wife, converting was more of a "Ruth scenario"- *Where you go I will go, and where you stay I will stay. Your people will be my people and your God my God (Ruth, 1:16).* She is a praying woman; she has had a women's ministry for 27 years. And she has prayed for our family and me every day; I mean every day. She is my Virtuous Woman and has been holding us together for 45 years.

After leaving New Haven, I took a different position with MDC in Chapel Hill and lived in Raleigh. The next year, we built a home outside of Chapel Hill in Chatham County. After leaving MDC, I worked at North Carolina Central University until I was recruited by the Center for Creative Leadership. That was what you call a "dream job." I worked there for 16 years traveling all over the world and doing what I loved to do best- teaching and training leaders. By then, I was a motivational speaker. I got to travel around the country to see how beautiful it is and how rich it is and how those riches are kept from some people.

A few people can move ahead quickly because they have wealth and others who move ahead quickly because they work hard and have unique talents. I learned that in the end, everything is about wealth and power and who holds it. People use different religious facades to cover this fact, but in the end, wealth and who holds it trumps everything else.

Along with the rest of the brothers in this book, I purpose to pass on wisdom to the younger brothers. I mentor 7-10 young men each year. Along with my business partner, we have set up Nehemiah-The Leadership Company in Greensboro, N.C. We are in the business of Building People for Effective Leadership.

I Still Laugh When I Think About It

Although some of the stories my father told were told to teach us life's lessons, many stories were simply to entertain. Before we owned a television and for years afterward- our local station signed off the air at 10:00 p.m. - Daddy's stories were our best form of entertainment. This story, like most of his stories, did a bit more than entertain.

****

I was twelve when it happened. Just started working in the fields. I tell you ain't no place this side of hell as hot as a South Carolina cotton field in mid-July. As children, it was our job to pick the leftover cotton.

All of a sudden someone screamed, "Luke done dropped dead." Everyone rushed over to see.

Now, we didn't pronounce him dead just cause he looked dead. We ran some scientific tests to make sure. Someone ran up to the house to get a mirror and held it in front of his nose. It didn't cloud up. Someone plucked a feather off of a hen and held it in front of his nose. The feather didn't move one bit. Uncle Luke was pronounced really and surely dead.

Some of the men picked the body up and carried him up to his house and laid him on the front stoop until they could build a box for him. His wife gave the men a length of cloth that she was saving to make a dress for Big Meeting[2] at the church. They used it to line the box before they washed him and dressed him in his Sunday-go-to-meeting suit. They placed the box in the front room of his house for the Wake that evening.

Back then, Wakes had a real purpose. People would stay awake all night and sit with a body to make sure that the supposed dead person didn't wake-up before they were put in the ground. During the summer, Wakes didn't last more than a day and a night.

That evening everyone was sitting around eating and drinking and trying to think of some good things to say about Uncle Luke. You see, Uncle Luke was known for being the meanest, stingiest man in the Bottom. He was up in his fifties, and he had married this pretty fifteen-year-old gal. He made it known that he didn't want anyone- man, boy, or woman coming within 100 ft. of his house. The men and boys cause he was jealous and the women because he didn't want the women giving his wife any ideas contrary to his.

Well, finally someone stood up and said that they thought they saw, they wouldn't swear to it on the Bible, but they might have seen Uncle Luke put a dime in the church offering plate and only take back eight cents in change.

It got real quiet. No one could think of another good thing to say.

All of a sudden Uncle Luke sat up. Looked around at all the people and said, "What're yawl doing up in my house?"

Every mouth in the place dropped open.

We were at a Wake but ain't nobody ever seen a dead man wake up before.

I took off running. My cousin was right behind me, but since he was a year older and a lot more scared, he passed me. We didn't stop running until my cousin ran smack dab into a tree and tripped me into falling on top of him.

He's got a knot on his head the size of a walnut to this very day as proof of what happened that night.

As I sat at the Wake for my 57-year-old father, the longest hour of my entire life, I thought of that story when I noticed my father's cousin who did indeed have a knot on his forehead. I smiled through the tears.

[2] **Big Meeting** was the Sunday, usually afternoon service followed by a meal, that marked the end of Rival Week.

Leaving a Legacy

What Every Father Owes His Sons

Elder Timothy E. "Gene" Blackmon

Two months before I was born, my father went to prison. My mother moved back home to live with her parents. Her sister and her three children were already living there. So, I grew up in a household with three strong women helping to raise me. My cousins seemed more like brothers and sisters and my grandfather seemed more like a father than grandfather. Although they did not live in the same house, I also had my uncles as mentors and role models.

My mother went to college and had a very good job. So, I

can't say that I grew up poor or anything like that. The only thing that I felt that I missed out on was some kind of relationship with my father. When he got out of prison, he married someone else and started another family. Years later, we got to know each other, but our relationship will never be a true father-son relationship- we are more like acquaintances. Kind of like some of the people who I went to school with- I can remember seeing them in the halls, but I never really got to know them.

When I think about my father, I think about the kind of father I do not want to be. It's not so much that he went to prison, it's more because of the way he treated me after he got out of prison. I want to have a strong relationship with my son. I have given a great deal of thought to the kind of legacies I want to leave to my son.

There are three types of legacies that a father should leave for his family and community. One is spiritual, another is integrity, and the other is financial. Sometimes we get so involved in the life that we are living from minute to minute or day to day that we don't really plan or give any thought to the kind of legacy that we will leave behind.

Leaving a spiritual legacy is important because it gives us a foundation for us to have faith, to hope, and to be humble and still maintain our balance in life. When I say spiritual, I'm not talking about one particular religion, but about faith in some power beyond oneself. Basically, values and a belief system.

I think a legacy of integrity or character is important because when we live our lives trying to do what is right, we tend to make better choices for ourselves and our community. When our hearts are right, we tend to make choices that will help others in our community. Character is something that we can only teach our sons through our example. Talking about it doesn't mean a thing if we do not live with character before our sons.

Perhaps, the most important legacy that we can leave behind is a legacy of financial security and wealth. In our communities, it is often our financial legacy that we put off or never get around to investing in. Maybe, we give so little thought to our financial future because we are often unable to see beyond our current financial situation. When a person is living from day to day or from paycheck to pay to check, it's difficult to plan for the next generation. It is difficult but not impossible. I remember my grandmother keeping what she called her "little nest egg" and no matter how broke everyone else around her might be, she could go in her bedroom and come out with some money.

We don't talk very much about finances and handling money, but I guess that goes back to the fact that most of us have not had very much opportunity to deal with major finances. It's pretty hard to talk about something that you do not know very much about. That's why it's important to spend some time with people who have money and appear to have mastered how to manage it. Broke folks don't have any real financial information.

I believe that the final step in Civil Rights is financial empowerment and we must do that ourselves. Even before someone has a great deal of money, they can begin to take steps towards financial empowerment by taking a few simple steps. First, whatever amount of money a person has should be budgeted. Everyone should plan what they're going to do with every dime- rent, utilities, food, other bills, and entertainment.

The next step is planning for financial success. One of the things that one of my mentors taught me was planning what to do with my money in the long run. He said, "How are you going to empower yourself financially if you don't have a plan for your money?" I understood that he was not talking about the next pay check, but about the next one and all the ones after that. A financial plan is a kind of business plan in that you set goals and give a great deal of thought to how you are going to reach those goals.

In our community, we tend to make money and then it's gone. Get it, and it's gone. There is a reason why there are certain kinds of stores in every black community. They know that we have money. The issue is not making money; it is keeping the money. I read somewhere that African Americans spend more than a trillion dollars a year and most of it is not spent in our communities, and it's not in our bank accounts. If we are ever to become an empowered people, we must plan and spend our money in our communities.

Young people have to be taught how to manage their money. They don't teach it in school or church, and many young people do not learn it at home. If a child grows up in a home where they have to move every two months because their parents never pay the bills, they are not likely to know how to handle money. Our children need money management programs as much as they need reading programs.

Young people need to understand how significant it is for us to be homeowners and property owners. At one time, in our community, only very young couples rented. Renting was seen as a way to save money to own a home eventually. Most people don't know this, but rent is so high nowadays that it is cheaper in many cases to own your home. There are numerous "first-time" buyer programs that help even single people buy their first home. We have to stop looking at that first home as our "dream" home- our forever home. We have to think of it as a starting place- a first step to owning property. We also have to make the property that we own part of our financial legacy.

I have seen so many people in our community sell family land or homes so that family members could get a little piece of change, then watched that same property developed and sold for millions. Those millions could have stayed in their family if they'd kept the land and taken the time to plan what they wanted to do with it- what kind of legacy they wanted to leave to the next generation. My grandfather used to say, "Land is the only thing God isn't making any more of." That makes, even more, sense today when land is such a valuable commodity. The land is the most stable part of a person's wealth.

Usually, it's the simple things about managing money that trips us up. Sometimes we tend to focus on the things that we do not have financially, rather than thinking positively about our assets. No, most of us will never have parents or associates who can give us a few million to get started or bail us out when we make bad investments. What we do have in abundance are good ideas, sound educations, and skills that we have learned from working. Once we learn how to copyright and patent our ideas (This should always be done before looking for financing), we can begin to empower ourselves financially.

Another little thing that often messes up young entrepreneurs is trying to grow too fast and not putting most of the money that they make the first year or so that they are in business back into the business or in savings. I had a friend whose wife made hundreds of thousands of dollars the first couple of years in her combination beauty salon and day spa. They also spent hundreds of thousands of dollars-matching Mercedes Benzes, a five-bedroom house, season tickets to Panther's games, etc. Then, all of a sudden, a lot of black women started going natural. She went out of business because she did not manage her money so that she could convert her business to accommodate the new market.

Accumulated money and property is power. We will never be an empowered people until we have learned these things.

COUNCIL OF ELDERS & JO EVANS LYNN

About the Authors

Thomas Allan Bell was born and raised in Philadelphia, Pennsylvania. He graduated from North Carolina State University with a degree in Industrial Education. After graduating, he settled in Greensboro, North Carolina; married and raised his three children (two boys and one girl) in his adopted city. He is a member of Bethel AME Church. He has served as a mentor at several Elementary schools in the Guilford County School System.

Ezekiel Ben-Israel-A.K.A. Robert Benson Duren, II attended the Greensboro City Schools graduating from James B. Dudley High School in 1972. He served in the United States Air Force as a Conscientious Objector. Although he refused to carry a gun, he served honorably as an orderly at military hospitals in Texas and in Turkey. He has a B.A. in Industrial Technology, Manufacturing from North Carolina A&T State University and a M.S. in Counseling Psychology, Oral Roberts University. He is a Certified Counselor. He is a member and Associate Pastor at Trinity AME Zion Church.

Timothy E. "Gene" Blackmon, The youngest member of the *Council of Elders* is a licensed master barber with 20 years' experience. He is father of one son. He graduated from Page High School where he was a pitcher on the varsity baseball team. He is the founder of Prestige Barber College in Greensboro.

, a native of Dunn, North Carolina, and a graduate of North Carolina A&T State University. After graduation, he joined the United States Army as a Commissioned Officer. He served 25 years in the military. Throughout his career in the military, he volunteered to mentor and coach youngsters. He is the Executive Director of Hayes-Taylor Memorial YMCA in Greensboro, North Carolina.

McArthur Davis, a native of Winston Salem, North Carolina is the Executive Director of the S.A.V.E.D. Foundation which is a group of Behavioral Health & Social Service Providers. He is a certified Counselor and the father of two sons and one daughter. He has mentored with MenTors and the *Council of Elders*.

Milton "Choo Choo" Grady was born in Washington, D.C. at the Army Hospital. He was raised by his grandparents. He has a Bachelor of Science Degree from North Carolina A&T State University. The father of one son, he has been married for 45 years. For many years he has served as a community and youth advocate. Most of his job experience has been with nonprofits. He has mentored with BOTSO, MenTors, and the *Council of Elders*.

Arthur Johnson, Jr., a native of Charleston South Carolina retired from the United States Army after 22 years of service. He is also retired from the U.S. Post Office. Johnson is a member and Steward at Bethel AME Church in Greensboro. He has served as a mentor in the *Council of Elders*.

Lt. Col. Clifton Girard Johnson (Retired) graduated from James Benson Dudley High School in 1969. He graduated from A&T State University in 1974 with a B.S in Engineering. He also has a master's degree from Troy State. He served 25 years in the United States Air Force.

Rev. Alphonso McGlen, a native of Washington D.C. entered the ministry when he was 15 and was pastoring his first church at the age of 23. He entered the United

States Army as an enlisted man and later attended Howard University and the Seminary at Shaw University. As the pastor of Bethel AME Church in Greensboro, he became involved with the mentoring programs sponsored by several of his members.

Ralph D. Mitchell, a native of Madison, Wisconsin is a motivational speaker. He has degrees from Knoxville College and the University of North Carolina Chapel Hill. He served in the Infantry of the United States Army where he reached the rank of First Lieutenant. He worked for many years at the Center for Creative Leadership. Mitchell is the chairman of Nehemiah-The Leadership Company. He is a member of Mont Zion Baptist Church. He has been married 45 years and has two sons and five grandchildren.

David "Bunny" Moore, James B. Dudley Class of 1962, Member of the Dudley High School Drum Line and the A&T State University Drum Line. Moore is a long-time community activist, 2015 Inductee Dudley Hall of Fame, Winner 2015 Alumni Service Award, volunteer, and mentor for students throughout the Guilford County School System. Moore is one of the founding members of BOTSO, MenTors, and the *Council of Elders*. In each of the groups he has served as leader or president. David Moore has been married for 53 years and is the father of one daughter and two sons.

Robert "Bob" Purvis is a native of Williamson, North Carolina and he graduated from E.J. Hayes High School. He has been married 51 years and is the father of three children (Two boys and one girl). He retired from Boy Scouts of America after 17 years of service. He is a founding member of Faith Community Church in Greensboro.

James Aquilla Smith, one of the first African American SCCA Crew Chiefs has served as a mentor with MenTors, and the Council of Elders. He founded a program for youth in 1988, Youth for Truth, which focused on reading and career prep. He also volunteers with the James B. Dudley High School Electric Car Team.

Henry "Hank" Wall, a native of High Point, North Carolina was a member of one of the last classes to graduate from William Penn High School. He joined David Moore as one of the founding members of Bothers Organized to Save Others (BOTSO) and later mentored with MenTors and the *Council of Elders*. He served in the United States Army. Wall retired after 25 years of service from the United States Post Office. He continues to work with BOTSO; working with two chapters of the program in Greensboro and High Point, North Carolina.

John E. Wynn is a native of Greensboro who grew up in the Warnersville Community that was settled by former slaves and freedmen. He grew up a member of the African Methodist Episcopal Zion Church since early childhood. He served several tours of duty in the United States Army that took him to various places all over Europe. He says that he always made it a point to learn the language of the countries where he was deployed. After leaving the military, he worked for the government for 19 years. John has served as a mentor in BOTSO, MenTors, and with the *Council of Elders.* He was an active parent at Ben L. Smith High School, volunteering for over 10 years serving as president and vice-president of the PTA and the Athletic Boosters. He is the father of two sons and has been married for 35 years.

VI

COUNCIL OF ELDERS & JO EVANS LYNN

Co-Author's Notes

Dr. Jo Evans Lynn-

Growing up in the Morningside Homes Projects, in Greensboro, North Carolina, I developed a clear understanding of what it takes for an individual to move from poverty to success. I spent 37 years as an educator, a mentor, and a community activist.

In the men of the *Council of Elders*, I found more than a dozen people who share my passion for helping others.

Writing this book was a unique learning experience for me. I enjoyed and appreciated the opportunity to help the men of the *Council of Elders* bring their stories and their lessons about life to the current and future generations of Black men. I agree with them that their roles as mentors are essential to helping young Black men become empowered men of strength and character.

I grew up in a household with a father who was the ultimate alpha male of his day. He worked two or more jobs at the same time throughout his adult life. He served honorably in the military and he kept his trim military weight and the habit of having spit polished shoes for the rest of his life. He was quiet. So, when he spoke, we knew it was something that was important.

This poem from my collection of poems, *Walk of Faith*, is a tribute to my father.

In My Father's Hand

My hand
In my father's hand
Always comforted me.
This mighty colossus,
This slayer of giants,
This rebuker of the closet monsters
That peered out at me
With wooly browed, brass button eyes.
This killer of scary under the bed things,
Had hands as large as brogan shoes.
Strong callused hands,
That could reach down
And make me feel
Like an angel with wings
When he picked me up
For a ride on
Shoulders as broad as from here to California.

That metaphorical view of my father never changed even after I was old enough to realize that he was not perfect. I always knew that he was different in some ways from most of the other fathers of his generation. The man could cook and he didn't mind babysitting his kids when my mother had to stay overnight or go to the beach with the family for whom she worked as a combination maid/cook/nanny.

Although the public schools for Negroes in York, South Carolina only went through the sixth grade when my father was a boy, my father was better educated than some college professors. He loved to read and he often read aloud to us. He was a consummate storyteller and he put his own spend on every story. For example, I didn't find out until I started school that Cinderella wasn't a

Colored girl and her "prince" wasn't a doctor at L. Richardson Hospital.[3] Daddy was warm and loving when we were small and he was always the one who came to our rescue when we had a nightmare. I never outgrew calling him Daddy.

Perhaps, the way that my Daddy so uniquely defined the term "alpha male" for me is why it felt strange, at the age of 68, having my definition of the alpha male evolve and take on new dimensions as I wrote the stories of the men of the *Council of Elders*. Through the *Council of Elders,* I learned several important aspects of the *contemporary alpha male*. The *contemporary alpha male* is strong and sensitive to the needs of others. The *contemporary alpha male* still hustles to take care of his family. Today's alpha male is emotionally connected to his family, to his community and to his culture.

My primary contributions to the book were my appreciation of the Elders' roles as mentors and my ability to put the extensive interviews into narrative book form. The Elders and I consider this book to be our 'gift' to present and future generations of Black men.

[3] L. Richardson Hospital opened in 1926 as the first hospital for Blacks in Greensboro, North Carolina.

OTHER BOOKS BY JO EVANS LYNN

Set in rural South Carolina and urban North Carolina, in the novel **Holding On: A Parable of Faith and Strength**, we watch Sister Fullmore emerge through a very untypical childhood to become a very untypical woman. The book begins on her first day of school, where we see hints of the smart, sassy young woman she becomes.

Her grandma Hester tells her, "Pick your man, don't let a man pick you. That way you know what you're getting."

In all her sixteen years of living, Sister hasn't met one man who tempted her to forget that advice. Then she meets a fine piece of chocolate manhood named Joe Ervin Evans...

"This back is like stepping back and experiencing that time in our lives all over again. Her writing is so real. I loved it!" Toni Jordan

Walk of Faith is about living, growing, and walking in the light. Every poem invites the reader to laugh, cry, sing, and pray with the poet while taking a spiritual journey. Each poem speaks, rather than preaching, to the readers about the universal experiences of all who walk daily in their faith. Even the poem titled "Gentle Sermon" is spiritually and realistically insightful, rather than preachy.

The Promise of Friendship is a moving rendition (but probably autobiographical) of a young girl's life in a Southern inner-city during the early 1950s and 1960s. You will absolutely love Josephine! Her intelligence and quick wit lend the novel an unusual sense of humor that amuses and challenges the reader. The literary style and technique employed enhance the authenticity of the reality of the story. It's absolutely amazing!!! (*JoAnn Eason Williams, Reviewer, Gates County Index*)

All books available at AMAZON.com, or from your local book dealer.

The book is a comprehensive study of the education of African Americans in Greensboro, North Carolina, and Guilford County with primary focus on James Benson Dudley High School. The book is a unique combination of personal narratives from people who lived the history recounted in the book and a well-documented pictorial and factual account of an important time and place in African American history. The book begins with the Antebellum Era and continues through 2020.

"It was an amazing time to understand more about the history of Dudley. Your presentation of your book makes me enjoy my time at Dudley" (Lucimar Ramirez-Rodriquez)

Your book was the closest I've ever come to reading a "living" history about 'us'. Every time I pick it up, it reaffirms what a special place Dudley is." (Juliette "Judy" Jordan)

"I truly feel that this book should be in every Dudley graduate's personal library." (Brenda Thornhill Holmes)

Book available at AMAZON.com

The PA Book Review gave the book a 5-Star rating and said:

The uncomplicated writing and intimate storytelling will pull you into the book almost immediately. Born Grown is the biography of Travis C. Burrell that follows his journey from childhood through adulthood. The story unfolds with a 5-year-old Travis navigating the first day of school alone; he realizes that he does not come from a "typical" family. It continues to explore his life in foster homes and the complications and impact it had on him. The narrative is intensely personal and moving. It highlights how stifling and emotionally destructive neglectful homes are in a child's life. It occupies a child's mind and leaves a deep mark on his personality for the rest of his life. This book will make you feel deeply connected to the main character's struggles, adversities, and perseverance. It is heart-breaking yet hopeful and inspiring on another level. It uniquely enmeshes humor and sorrow. The authors will challenge your thoughts and views and make you understand how difficult and challenging life is for children in foster care; how it consumes all aspects of one's life. This book will resonate with you for a long, long time.

Born Grown: The Making of Travis C. Burrell should be required reading for any individual who hopes to work successfully with individuals from this target group. The book and discussion guides are available on Amazon.

Made in the USA
Columbia, SC
13 July 2021